How to Start and Run Your Own Word-Processing Business

Gary S. Belkin

The Wiley Press
John Wiley & Sons, Inc.
New York • Chichester • Brisbane • Toronto • Singapore

Publisher: Judy V. Wilson
Editor: Theron Shreve
Managing Editor: Katherine Schowalter
Electronic Book Publishing Services:
The Publisher's Network, Morrisville, PA

Library of Congress Cataloging in Publication Data

Belkin, Gary S.
   How to start and run you own word-processing business.

   Includes index.
   1. Word processing operations.   2. New business enterprises.   3. Home-based businesses.   I. Title.
HF5548.115.B44   1984   652   83-21691
ISBN 0-471-88396-4

To Melanie,

still the one

Table of Contents

Introduction

If you've ever thought about running your own business – especially a business from home – you know that you are faced with a multitude of questions and important decisions that may seem staggering. How do I get started? Where do I get customers and where should I advertise? Should I rent a small office nearby or run the business out of my home? How do I finance the business and support myself until it starts bringing in money? How do I structure my prices so they are competitive and profitable? Is there really a market out there for what I have to offer? Which services are most profitable and which are least profitable? How do I get the technical and practical information I need to keep up with my competitors?

How To Start and Run Your Own Word-Processing Business answers these questions and more. It offers you detailed information about how to start-up your own word processing business with a minimum of capital investment and shows you how to run it on a day-to-day basis, efficiently and economically. In addition to learning what word processing is, how it works, and its importance in business and commerce, you will learn in the following pages how to use your personal, technical, and business skills and contacts to attract clients, to help finance the equipment you need, and to turn your time and effort into rewarding profits. Moreover, the book has many practical examples and specific suggestions to follow if you are:

- the owner of a word processor or microcomputer (Radio Shack, Apple, IBM, Kaypro, Eagle, Columbia, Morrow, Victor, etc.), who is considering running a part-time or full-time word processing business from home.
- a college student, secretary, administrative assistant, typist, or temporary office worker looking to make an independent career with a word processing business.
- a business professional – attorney, small business owner, accountant, insurance or real estate salesperson, securities dealer, or an academic – who wants to use a microcomputer to generate extra income or wants a return on their investment.
- a school teacher who wants to parlay newly acquired word processing skills into a profitable, low-risk, after-school, summer, or weekend business.

The book begins by introducing and surveying the entire field of word processing. It progresses from simple definitions of what a word-processing system is, to the latest applications of electronic data base retrieval. The material presented assumes that you have no previous knowledge of computers or information processing. If you already know something about word processing you will still find many concepts clarified and some practical hints about how to select hardware and software that can make your business run more efficiently. A glossary in the back of the book will help acquaint you with any technical terms you come across.

After the introduction to the field of word processing, you will find specific procedures for beginning your business from scratch – and managing it once it gets going. You will find suggestions for deciding on your business location, anticipating (and controlling) your overhead, budgeting yourself, keeping records, hiring and training operators. You will also be advised how to avoid some of the common problems that plague new businesses.

In chapter 6, we go beyond word processing to explore how you can use your talents to offer highly profitable services in conjunction with your word processing business. You will see how to assemble mailing lists, prepare letters and resumes, offer business management and support services, and use your word processor as a gatherer of information from distant sources.

We begin with a general survey of what word processing is, and look at some of the better opportunities available.

1

What Is Word Processing?

In 1980, Patricia Gibson was typing five to eight hours a day at home. She was taking care of her one-year-old daughter while her husband, Robert, went off each day to teach at a junior high school (a job he had lost enthusiasm for years ago). Linda Marchand was working long and, for her, unrewarding hours as a manager at Saks, a prestigious New York department store. All her friends thought it was a great job, but Linda longed for independence and freedom from the drudgery of nine-to-five life. Valentina Ciletti was completing her undergraduate training as an elementary school teacher and earning tuition money by typing term papers on weekends and at night. In her senior year she realized she did not want to be a teacher, but she didn't like typing either. After ten years of working, Stephanie Abrams was not enjoying her family life as a full-time homemaker and mother. When her daughter, Lauren, reached school age, she felt pressed by the thought of having to go out to work again, but the family really needed her extra income.

Within two years, the lives of these four people changed radically in ways they would never have imagined.

Robert and Patricia Gibson started first one, and then two successful word-processing and copy centers. While they were still in their early forties they went into semi-retirement. They were able to live on the income from their businesses, which now ran themselves. Linda Marchand began her own successful word-processing business, *Words to Go*, which she ran from her home. The business provided her with a higher income than she had ever earned before. Valentina Ciletti was earning over eighteen dollars an hour running her own word-processing operator training program from office space she rented a few blocks from her apartment. And, Stephanie Abrams was earning more per hour working part-time at home preparing material for publishing firms than she had earned at her previous job.

Each of these individuals found that word processing offered more business and growth opportunities than their previous positions. They could work at home or rent space; they could run their business by themselves or hire operators; they could work full-time or part-time; and, most importantly, they could be their own bosses. And, they succeeded: within a year they were able to give up jobs they didn't want to fully enjoy the fruits of their labors.

THE WORD-PROCESSING REVOLUTION

The word-processing revolution is upon us. Those who join early are finding that the rewards are rich. Throughout the country, homemakers, secretaries, teachers, creative individuals in the arts, and many others who want to start a business are finding exciting opportunities in word processing. They are discovering that the enormous capabilities and relatively low cost of microcomputers allow them to provide a wide range of services. Microcomputers also enable them to exploit their personal skills and competencies, and offer far more than any typist or secretary could.

If you think that word processing is just a fancy kind of typing, think again. With today's modern word-processing equipment, you can become a provider and manager of information. You can produce multi-color graphs and charts from a table of statistics your client gives you. Information can be gathered through your word processor and sold to clients. You can dial a data bank (such as a customer mailing list, an inventory file, a stock market quotation, or a list of relevant legal citations) and, without ever leaving the keyboard, merge this information with any kind of text (letters, contracts, briefs, dissertations, etc.) or convert it into graphic form. Drafts can be run off on a high-speed printer and distributed to several readers simultaneously. Corrections can then be made, and final letter-quality copy typed perfectly at a page per minute. All this at considerably less expense than the cost of manual research and typing. Even if you already know word processing, you will learn how to go beyond the limits of typing, editing, and printing to offer your clients a range of services made possible by the versatality of modern word-processing equipment.

Yes, the word-processing revolution is already here. It arrived in the form of exciting new equipment (specifically the new breed of inexpensive microcomputers) and second generation software. Easy-to-use, fully assembled word-processing packages are readily available and basically inexpensive. You can, in fact, equip yourself with a pretty decent system for about three thousand dollars. Yet there are hundreds of thousands of offices throughout the country that have let the revolution pass them by. They remain stuck in the age of manual typing and manual filing tediously revising documents, with painfully slow record-keeping and filing procedures. It is these offices that will need your business.

The Technologically Naive

Why, you ask, do so many business offices continue to use typewriters? Why are electric and electronic typewriters still the norm in the majority of small offices in the United States? Why, moreover, don't these people who type at home for a living switch in droves to word processors? And why are there still so many classified ads in the paper for typists – and so many people responding? Typing jobs pay less, are more difficult, and hold far less prestige and fewer opportunities for advancement than do word-processing jobs. Typing is boring and repetitive; tiring and frustrating. Word processing is not.

The answers to these questions are the same: home typists, office personnel, and small business managers are under the mistaken impression that word processing is:

1. too complicated to learn;
2. too expensive to buy and maintain;
3. cost-effective only for large offices or businesses.

All these assumptions are false. In fact:

1. it is no more complicated to learn a word processor than it is to learn to type – in fact it takes less time;
2. the cost of word-processing power has come down so much over the past five years that, counting hours of labor costs and productivity benefits, it is actually less expensive today to use a word processor than to use a typewriter;
3. word processing is now suitable for and applicable to any business, regardless of size, and most individuals who use a typewriter regularly.

So, let's look briefly at the origins of word processing

and at the components that make up today's word-processing systems, and see what is necessary to start your own business.

DEVELOPMENT OF WORD PROCESSING

The origins of word processing bring together the history of the typewriter, the growth of the small computer, and the fruits of a new science called *ergonomics* – the study of technological design that focuses on the human being interacting with the machine. A word processor is basically an electronic typewriter and a computer combined, with a few small but critical ergonomic modifications.

The first modern version of the typewriter was introduced in the late 19th century by Christopher Shoales. He was a Milwaukee inventor who is generally credited with making the first practical typewriter, although others developed similar machines at the same time. As an instrument, it had a profoundly democratizing effect: it made the written output of the lawyer, client, professional writer, reader, publisher, critic, carper, letter writer, or common individual identifiably uniform. As long as one had access to a typewriter, one's words and ideas would appear as neat, as professional, and as formal as anyone else's.

While we take this for granted today, it has had, and continues to have, a revolutionary impact on the way we think about words and the discrepant way we treat typed versus hand-written material. This is why the person working from home today can generate professional word-processing output that is identical in appearance with, and be received just as favorably as, that generated in the elegant offices of Fortune 500 corporations. The uniformity of the typed medium gave power to the home typist in the same way that the development of printing gave power to anyone with a press and something to say.

With the introduction of electric typewriters in the 1950s, and the phenomenal growth of selectric type-element typewriters in the 1960s and early 1970s, typing was thought to be on the technological advance. Actually, these innovations did practically nothing to increase typing speed. Most typists, in fact, only increased their speed a few words per minute with the electric typewriters.

While electric typewriters did not do much for increased capacity, they did have two important effects. First, a typist could type accurately – and without mental or physical fatigue – for a much longer period of time. While a skilled typist could type approximately 3.5 hours on a manual, after three weeks of training and practice with an electric, the same typist could type about twice as long with the same error ratio.

Also, continuing the trend toward democratization of the nonprinted written medium, the new typewriters gave a better, more consistent, uniform output. Typist fatigue did not show, characters did not smudge, and the q and h (struck with left pinkie and right index fingers respectively) were now equally as dark and firm on the paper. With the new "carbon" ribbons, proportional spacing machines, lift-off correcting tape and changeable elements, typing output began to look as if it were printed. The quality of typed manuscript was coming remarkably close to that of the printed book. Because of this development, a camera-ready book, that will be acceptable in many types of publishing markets, can be generated from a relatively modest microcomputer or word processor.

In the 1960s, IBM introduced a typewriter that could store the information typed on magnetic tape: the MTST (Magnetic Tape Storage Typewriter). This is generally considered the first "real" word processor. Like today's more advanced machines, the process consisted basically of keyboarding information into the system, having it stored, and then having it typed back on demand. But, you couldn't edit what you typed and you couldn't preview material until it was typed. The storage was also extremely limited.

The tape system did not work well for several reasons. First, tape is very slow and retrieving information took a long time. Second, tape always has to be played in sequence; that is, to get to the third page you have to first go through pages one and two. Also, if you want to add a long block to page three, the entire tape has to be reformatted.

In the early 1970s the *floppy disk* was introduced. This flexible piece of plastic is approximately the size of a 45 rpm record. It is housed permanently in a protective jacket, which is inserted into the disk drive with its spinning hub. The information is stored in the form of magnetic signals, as it is stored on cassettes or mag cards. But, as with a phonograph record, you could access information in any order you wanted. This came to be called *random access storage*.

About the same time the new disks were being introduced, another important innovation occurred. The CRT (cathode ray tube) screen, which had already gained wide application in the computer field, was now being used with word-processing machines. The size of the screens varied, but the Vydec 1146, introduced in the early 1970s, allowed an operator to see a full legal size (64-line) page at a time. What this meant in practice was that an operator no longer had to sit through the slow process of printing out a long document to see what was stored. Instead, by moving a single point – called a cursor – the operator could get to any place on the page he or she wanted. This increased the editing capabilities enormously, and made the editing process much simpler.

All these developments would not have been of much consequence if the integrated circuits and microprocessing "chips" had not become widely available and relatively inexpensive. Electronic miniaturization allowed a complex series of commands (software) to be stored in a relatively small amount of space. This made it possible for machines to display, edit, print, store, and process a wide range of documents in various ways – from two line memos to multi-page fill-in forms and ledger sheets.

All these developments combined form, the basis for today's typical word-processing system. Some systems are all-purpose microcomputers, (such as an *IBM PC*, *Apple Macintosh* or *TRS-80*) suitable for word processing as well as many other tasks. Others are "dedicated" word processors which, although they may be used for other types of applications, have been designed from the bottom up for the processing of words and documents (machines like *Lanier*, *Micom*, *Xerox*, *IBM Displaywriter*, *Vydec*, *CPT*, and *Wangwriter*).

WHAT DO WE MEAN
BY WORD PROCESSING?

Word processing is a part of a larger field called *electronic information processing*. This broader term refers, in fact, to a wide range of different electronic office machines, including copiers, computers, teletypes, telephone switchboards, dictation equipment, microfilm readers, and more. What all these have in common is that they store, process, or transmit information. They may do so over special lines in the office, over phone lines or may perform these functions in different ways; inside their own containers. The output may be different; a printed sheet, a photocopy, some information on a video screen, or a ringing telephone. But in all these cases, some information is moved and changed.

Electronic information processing includes both *word processing* and *data processing*. From the point of view of the person designing and building the equipment, there is generally little difference between the two. In fact, some of the leading word-processing units on the market today were originally designed as data processing units. However, from the point of view of the user – the person whom the machine is serving – the differentiation is important. For the user, the differences between word processing and data processing are found in the kinds of information put in and taken out of the machine. Differences can also be found in the ways of inputting, in formatting options and what one can do with the information, as well as the printed quality of the output.

Text vs. Data

For simplicity, we can say that word processing is concerned with *textual* material while data processing is concerned with *numerical* material. Textual material is that material which is made up of strings of alphanumeric characters, (that is, the letters from a to z and the characters 1–9 and 0), recognizable as units of what can be called the *printed language hierarchy*. This hierarchy, in order, consists of:

Letter (Character)
Word
Line
Sentence
Paragraph
Page
Document

If you pick up a book, correspondence, or any type of written material, you can immediately recognize the elements of this hierarchy. If I say, "Go to the fourth word on the third line of this page," your finger can move about as quickly as I can say it. This recognition of elements is central to the editing of any written material where one is asked to change (that is; add to, delete from, or replace with other) characters, words, lines, sentences, and paragraphs. Any machine that is to help us edit text, therefore, must be able to quickly and easily recognize these units – or at least most of them – and must allow the operator to quickly and directly get to a letter, a word, a line, etc.

Electronic Editing: Making the Most of Words

Let's say I want to switch around two paragraphs, making the first paragraph the second, and the second the first. This task would be quite simple for any typist to understand. But, for a general computer – even the most sophisticated and up-to-date – an enormous amount of programming information is required for recognizing, pointing to, moving a paragraph around, and then pushing all the other text forward. Even to program a computer to recognize what a word is, and then to be able to insert words in between other words, is a big programming job.

To do the same kinds of changes – moving a paragraph around or inserting a letter in a word – on a dedicated word processor or on a personal computer with good word processing software, requires approximately seven keystrokes and takes about six seconds. That's because the machine can make the recognition and follow the instructions quickly and accurately. A word processor has, built into its instructions, the kinds of recognitions and manipulations of the printed language hierarchy that a typist would understand. To sum up, then, any decent word processor must, at least:

- allow you easy typing input, with a keyboard that simulates a typical typewriter.
- allow you to access and change quickly any unit of the printed language hierarchy (add, delete or change letters, words, lines, etc.).
- allow you to reformat your page, in terms of margins, indentations, line spacing, etc.

- provide you with an attractive-looking printed (typed) output of your document in either draft or final stages.

In addition, most of today's word processors allow you to do many more things, such as detect and correct spelling errors, merge mailing lists with form letters, keep an updated list of your appointments and key dates, index and footnote your documents automatically, and much, much more. It is the *software* that makes all these things possible when you are using a personal computer.

Software – The Key to Word Processing Power

Software is the series of instructions that tells a computer what to do. You buy a word-processing software package – such as WordStar™, Perfect Writer™, Peachtext™ or EXECUTIVE SECRETARY™ – and load the program into the computer memory by pressing a button. The series of computer language instructions (the program) makes it possible for the machine to do whatever it is programmed to do, transforming an ordinary microcomputer into a word processor.

SELECTING YOUR SOFTWARE

Ultimately, the quality and utility of any word processor is found in the software. Ideally, you should really decide on your software before you buy your physical machine – your hardware, as it is called. Many people make the mistake of buying their hardware first and then finding out that the software available for that machine is not the software that is best suited for their specific purposes. A central part of your decision about which computer or word processor to buy should be the software that is compatible. A given piece of software generally "fits" only one type of

machine, although some popular word-processing software packages come in many different versions.
Word processing software is sold in a package that consists of:

- a floppy disk with the machine-coded instructions (the program);
- a manual that explains how the program works (the documentation);
- *A* sometimes another floppy disk, which is used as a tutorial for training you to use the software;
- and possibly a card entitling you (for a fee) to a support arrangement through which you can get help from the publisher, over the phone, if you have any questions regarding how the software works.

You can generally evaluate word processing software on four criteria:

1. how well it does what it is supposed to do (its performance);
2. how well-designed it is to avoid "crashing" (forcing you to shut down the computer and restart the whole process;
3. how good the "fail-safe" features are that prevent the permanent loss of your text because of some small mistake by the user (error handling);
4. how compatible it is with other word-processing support programs, such as spelling checkers, data base managers, spreadsheets, graphics, and mailing list programs; and,
5. how easy it is to learn and use.

The last point requires a special caveat. Many of the programs that are most difficult to learn prove most adequate in the long run. A program's complexity generally means a more thorough and efficient program. Many programs that are simpler to learn are not powerful enough in the long run for serious word processing. Don't be tempted by a program that you can master in ten minutes – if there is such a thing. Once the satisfaction of having learned it fades, you will find that there are many features missing that you really could have used had you been willing to put in more time for training.

The ideal then, is a program that will allow you to meet as many demands as may arise in the course of your business. If a client wants you to print out a wide chart with a lot of figures in different columns, you want software that will support multi-column formatting and wide-screen printing. When a client wants a professionalized letter sent to a thousand people, and you want to be able to use the client's computer disks as your mailing list: you want software that can easily handle ZIP coding, sorting, and integration of the list into a text letter. If a client wants a doctoral dissertation with computer graphics, you want software that can support a graphics printer.

The Modern Word-Processing System

The modern word processing system consists of five main parts, whether it is an all-purpose microcomputer (Apple, IBM, Commodore, Texas Instruments, Radio Shack) with special word-processing software (Applewriter™, Perfect Writer, WordStar, or Scripsit™) or if it is a machine dedicated specifically to word-processing applications. These elements are illustrated in figure 1.1:

The Keyboard
The Monitor
The Storage Device
The Printer
The Processor

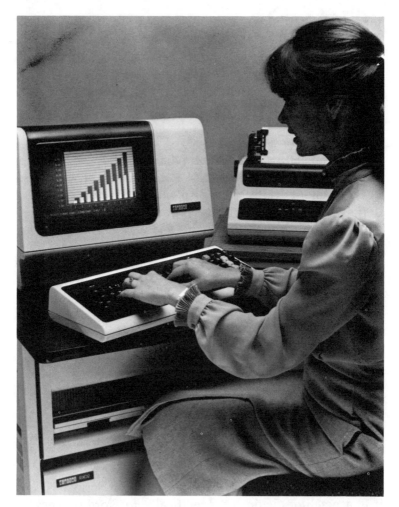

Courtesy of Digital Equipment Corporation

Figure 1.1 A typical word-processing system consists of a keyboard, monitor, storage device, printer, and processing unit (here, located below the table surface).

All the parts except the last one, are clearly visible to the user and may be directly examined. But the processing itself—through which most of the "magic" of word processing is accomplished—is done deep inside the machine, hidden from view, on tiny silicone chips. The processing comprises one, or several, circuit boards through which electronic signals transform your commands into actions and format text to your specifications.

The following two chapters discuss all these parts in detail, with special emphasis on how to make a purchase selection suitable to your needs—including buying a new system or upgrading your existing system. But for now, we shall briefly survey the main parts of the system to help you better understand what word-processing is, how it saves time and increases productivity.

The Keyboard

The word-processing keyboard is basically like a typewriter keyboard, with a number of "extra" keys. From machine to machine, these extra keys may differ, but some common extra keys include:

Cursor Control Keys. Usually four directional arrows (up ↑, down ↓, left ←, right →) that move the cursor around the screen to reach text that you want to change. On many microcomputers, the directional arrows are controlled by the *software* you are working with—not by the machine—therefore, unless you are working with the right software, they may not work when you press them.

Numeric Keys. The numeric keypad sits on the right side of the keyboard and looks like a calculator keyboard. This extra keypad is especially useful in accounting and statistical applications where numbers have to be frequently keyed into a document. The numbers on the top row of the standard keyboard can be used for numeric entry, but when there is a separate numeric keypad, it is much faster, less tiring, and more accurate to key in numbers.

Editing Keys. These keys may be labeled LINE OUT, CHARACTER DELETE, INSERT, WORD ENTER, BOLD FACE, etc. They are more often found on dedicated word processors than on microcomputers. By pressing them, you immediately instruct the machine to perform the function and eliminate the need to learn codes and routines to accomplish common word-processing applications.

System Keys. These keys marked PRINT, SAVE, WRITE, STORE, READ, etc. allow you to give instructions to the system in order to manage your work. They may allow you to transfer material to your storage medium, to read material from storage, to print material in a desired format and to perform a variety of other processes.

Function Keys. These are general all-purpose keys, (usually labeled F1, F2, F3, etc.) that, depending on the software, can perform a large number of functions. Many word-processing software programs now use function keys to speed up the input and editing of data. For example, if you are editing and you want to delete large blocks, pressing F1 may make all your deletions, paragraph by paragraph. If you want to delete one character at a time, pressing F2 may get you back into the character-deletion mode. Function keys add a great deal of versatility.

In addition to these keys, there may be any number of other special keys which will enable you to perform different procedures. Computer keyboards typically contain CTRL (Control) and ESC (Escape) keys, which we will talk about later. Sizes of keyboards vary greatly. Some having as few as 53 keys while others have up to 100.

The Monitor

The monitor technically called the CRT (cathode ray tube), is more commonly referred to as a screen. It makes the job of word processing immeasurably easier by making the visible input appear "fluid", that is, capable of being changed, edited, reformatted, and moved around on the screen. Also, by allowing the operator to see what the final product will look like before printing, the monitor saves a lot of unnecessary printing time.

Monitors always come as standard equipment in a dedicated word-processing system, but may be bought as a separate purchase when setting up a microcomputer system. The size and color of the screens vary. Typically screens are 7-inch to 12-inch, measured diagonally. They may feature green, white, or amber characters on a black background. The quantity of letters and lines on the screen, as well as their size and formation, may depend on the software—the word-processing program—and not strictly on the screen itself. It is quite conceivable that a 7-inch screen may display 25 lines of 80 characters each, while a larger screen may only display 17 lines of 40 characters.

The Storage Device

When the word processor is turned off, the memory is erased and all the material you have been writing or editing dies with it. Permanent external storage of your documents, therefore, is essential to making a word-processing system efficient: it allows you to recall and review your material at any time. The storage function in virtually all modern word processing systems is delegated to the *floppy disk*, which comes in two sizes: 8-inch square or 5.25-inch square (a newer 3-inch floppy is on the way). This flexible piece of plastic stores information in the form of magnetic signals. The disk is housed permanently in a protective jacket, which is inserted into the spinning disk drive, like a record on a turntable.

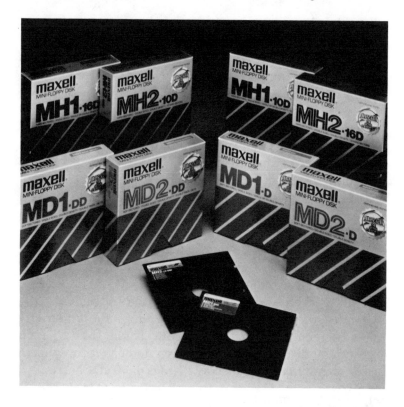

Courtesy of Maxell Corporation

Figure 1.2 The 5.25-in. floppy disks have become the standard for word-processing storage, although 8-in. disks are still widely used, especially on the dedicated word processors, such as the Vydec. Each disk can store between 40 to 100 pages of single-spaced typing.

The floppy disk brings together the chief advantages of both magnetic recording tape and the phonograph record. With a phonograph record, we can play the songs in any order we wish, skipping any songs along the way or playing some over. The material stored on a floppy disk can also be played, or retrieved, in any order we want it: from the beginning, middle, or end; or from any document or page anywhere on the disk. We do not have to go through pages 1 and 2 to view, on the screen, edit or print information stored on page 3. This convenience is called *random access memory* (RAM).

Unlike a phonograph record, on which the information is stored permanently and cannot be changed, the floppy disk, like magnetic recording tape, can be erased or recorded over. Thus, it has the advantage of a tape: it is capable of being reused over and over as we make changes, of storing newer and later revisions of our material over the old.

The Printer

The printer is responsible for the final output. It produces what our clients ultimately see and judge us by. It must, therefore, be uncompromisingly attractive in its printing appearance. And, because time is money, it should also be fast. Therein comes the compromise.

While a dot-matrix printer (where each letter is composed of tiny dots) is very fast (80–200 or more characters per second), the print quality is not generally acceptable for professional word-processing applications. Most word-processing systems, therefore, use daisy wheel printers. These printers spin a plastic or metal 96-spoke print wheel, which is struck by a printing hammer at a rate of 12 to 55 characters per second. That translates into the ability to print a single spaced legal page (8.5 x 13) in a little over a minute. This produces the best output possible and is reasonably fast.

A much faster way to print high-quality output, but

more expensive than daisy wheel printing, is ink-jet printing. This method shoots a stream of ink through an electronic grid. The ink lands on the paper, letter by letter, producing a very high-quality output. But the ink-jet technology is not always reliable and is quite expensive.

The Processor

Invisible to the user, the microprocessor is the heart of the microcomputer or word-processing system. The architecture of the processor and the way it works is of little or no concern to the user. The software that "runs" on the system—the series of instructions that tell the processor how to do the word processing—depends on the microprocessor. There are several different kinds of microprocessors and each one has its own set of rules and regulations (assembly language instructions). Purchasing a system that uses a popular processor generally opens the way to a larger variety of software than purchasing a system that uses a more obscure one. The chief microprocessors used today are: Z80, 6502, 8088, 8086, 6800, 68000. All of these are reliable and have been well-tested over the years. All of them also enjoy a large library of available software to make them useful for you.

The Operating System

The operating system (also called the disk operating system, or DOS) is a special software program that comes with your word-processing or microcomputer hardware. It is the main library of commands on which all the software that runs on the computer depends. You might think of it as the vocabulary of a language from which novels, plays, and poems are written.

In effect, the DOS is a series of machine language instructions that enables you to do all things you would expect to do with a computer: store or retrieve information from the disks; see text on the screen; print text; make copies of files; read a directory or catalog of what's on your disk, and more. In short, the operating system runs your computer for you.

The operating system may be an important consideration in selecting your computer, even though you will probably rarely have to deal with it. However, since software written for one operating system will not work on another operating system, it is something to consider. A widely used operating system will allow you to use many popular programs. For instance, if you own a Kaypro computer you can use many of the programs written in CP/M for dozens of other computers on the market. The four main disk-operating systems that dominate the market today, in order of popularity, are: Apple DOS, PC DOS, MS DOS, CP/M, and TRSDOS (Radio Shack). Any of these operating systems will assure you the use of a wide range of business and word-processing software, but each has its own strengths and limitations (see chapter 3). Incidentally, many microcomputers and word processors offer, as an option, a special board that will make the computer compatible with an operating system other than the one that comes with it. You should inquire about the costs for this board, however, since this option may add a significant amount to your purchase price. Also, as you will see in chapter 2, the promise of compatibility and the reality of a functioning, compatible system are often two quite different things.

2

Choosing
Your
Software

In chapter 1, we looked at word processing as a viable, new business opportunity. We also outlined some of the ways word processing can increase productivity and save money for both businesses and individuals. In this chapter, we'll begin by taking a more detailed look at the range of services you can provide, and then focus on the software that will enable you to provide these services.

If you are already using a word-processing system, or have already purchased a microcomputer, this chapter should help you to understand its strengths and limitations. If you have not yet purchased hardware or software for your business, this chapter will help you focus on the types of services you want to provide, and point out some of the available software that will support these services.

THE WORD-PROCESSING
WAY TO SUCCESS
SOME APPLICATIONS AND EXAMPLES

Once your word-processing system is installed and running, it can do much more than just word processing. In fact you will discover that its versatility is remarkable. Your personal skills and talents will determine exactly what you do with all its built-in capabilities. You should be aware, however, that your word-processing system has many, innovative, money-making applications.

One colleague of mine, who began by typing manuscripts at home, soon turned her hobby (pedigree dog breeding) into a word-processing related business. How? She bought a program for her Morrow Decision microcomputer that, with slight modification, enabled her to keep multigenerational pedigree records for the dogs she was breeding and selling. Hearing about this, some of her colleagues asked her to help them set up their records. Since she really didn't want to do this because the time would detract from her word-processing business, she asked for an unreasonably high fee for the service. But they were glad to pay this fee – and even sent more customers. In a short time, she was making as much doing this as she was with the word-processing business – and it took less time. Her word-processing skills enabled her to generate pedigree reports and documentation second to none, and the business boomed.

She is a good example of a person who turned her personal interests into profits using the microcomputer she had bought for word processing. In the following pages note some of the things the computer can do and try to decide which ones are compatible with your abilities.

Information and Research

Most businesses, as well as most individuals working

on reports and dissertations, need key facts, specific information, and data in order to work effectively. An insurance agent working on a big, multi-state deal might want to know about insurance supervision and regulations in North Dakota and Wyoming. A producer of packaging materials might want to know if any articles have been published showing the effects of safety packaging on sales of cosmetics. A doctoral student in comparative literature might want a comprehensive bibliography of all the articles about, and references to, the writer Elias Canetti.

Typically, this type of information would have to be laboriously researched through the indexes, abstracts, and reference works in large libraries, perhaps for days or weeks. This would certainly present a problem for the business or individual in a hurry. Since the pressure and demand on time is enormous, individuals who require information and research assistance are generally willing to pay a high price for it.

In the past, an information and research assistant would be an entirely different person from a word-processing operator. Nowadays, however, information searches by microcomputer – what we call an *online search* – bring together the technology of the microcomputer, and the printing and formatting functions of the word processor. This not only simplifies the process enormously – cutting down what used to take weeks to only minutes – but allows a far greater range of information to reach us. It also opens the door for intelligent, logical-thinking, word-processing operators to become online research assistants.

All you need to run your own online search service, in addition to your word-processing equipment, is a modem, some software, and a telephone. In chapter 6, you will see how to install and get online information service capabilities running. You will also learn where to get a two-day training course in this lucrative area.

Correspondence and Mailing List Services

Anyone in the process of starting a new business, or expanding a customer base, will probably consider sending out a mass mailing. Ideally, a professional-looking, individually typed letter, on personalized letterhead, will be used. In some cases clients will supply the mailing list and letterheads; in other cases you will have to assemble them for your clients.

With a word processor or microcomputer, you can obtain comprehensive, targeted mailing lists online (over the telephone). They can be stored permanently on your floppy disks for future jobs. You can also have multiple, standard business letters stored on disks—even different versions of the same letter for different types of business or fund raising situations. Once you store these letters in your computer you can easily and quickly merge them with your mailing lists to produce individually typed letters. If you have the ability to write a clear and effective business letter, you will see, in chapter 6, how to provide a low-cost, high-profit letter-writing and mailing service.

Resume Preparation

The resume is becoming an important factor in today's climate of increasing job mobility and changing employment opportunities. Most individuals seek professional help to get the best resume possible. You can learn how to prepare an effective resume (it takes only a few hours to learn the basic rules) and capitalize on this growing need by building a lucrative resume-preparation service.

The beauty of a resume-preparation business is that you make money at both ends. You charge for preparing the resume and for typing it into the word processor; then charge for every copy that is run off. Since it has to be typed into the system only once, and the printing is relatively fast, this is a highly profitable business. In chapter 4 we will look at the details of how to build a resume-preparation business.

Business Data Management

Keeping accurate business records – who received which order, who owes what for how long – is essential for a smooth operation. While larger businesses generally have their own accounts receivable and accounts payable departments, the small business operator often keeps records on a less formal basis.

To keep business records current and to be able to retrieve the information, requires a data base management system, combined with an accounting package. This is a program (software) which enables you to store records on your system's floppy disks and to generate billings and order sheets. If you have some knack for accounting or bookkeeping, you can transform your word processor or microcomputer into a mini-accounting system. You can combine your word-processing jobs with billing, orders, and record-keeping.

Graphics and Presentation

The ability to put complex data and statistics into easy-to-understand graphic formats is one of the great advantages of the microcomputer. In any kind of business promotion or report, a good graphics presentation makes a positive impression because it renders complex ideas and cumbersome data in an easy-to-understand format. For many business and professional people, the task is cumbersome. It involves either hiring a free lance graphics artist or tracing small accurate lines and circles by hand with fine pens and calibrated rulers. If you can provide this service economically, you can give a nice boost to your business oriented word-processing services. You will see, in chapter 6, how to promote all phases of your business using your graphics and presentation capabilities.

Other Opportunities

In addition to the functions previously mentioned, you can use your word processor to develop related businesses, according to your interests and abilities. Here are some ideas that may work well for you.

- Training word-processing operators is a lucrative field for those who enjoy working with people and who like to teach.
- Fund-raising organizations often depend on computers and word processors, which contain mailing lists, and can easily generate the tremendous amount of correspondence required. If you write well and can make the right contacts, you can provide these services.
- The preparation of legal documents, such as wills and real estate contracts, is done almost entirely on word processors today. If you can build a client base of lawyers, and learn some legal terms, preparing these documents can be a full-time job.

As you learn about word processing and microcomputers in this and the following chapters, you may want to begin a self-analysis that will help you determine where to channel your energies in starting and running your own word-processing business. Since the word-processing field offers so many opportunities in so many different areas, you can assess which aspects of the business are most suitable for you.

Because the heart of your business operations will depend on your word-processing software, we will begin with a detailed discussion of how to evaluate and select the best word-processing software for your needs.

YOUR WORD-PROCESSING SOFTWARE

A word-processing system consists of machines and peripherals (the computer, disk drives, printer, & modem) called the hardware, the word-processing program called the software, and the operator who makes it all work. In this section we will look at the software, which is the logical basis of word-processing operations. It should be considered before purchasing your hardware, since most word-processing software is specific to certain machines or operating systems, and will not run on different kinds of hardware. If you already own a microcomputer you might want to review this section to see if your system is state-of-the-art or if it can be substantially upgraded by making a small investment in some new software.

The overall performance of a system by far outweighs the sum of its parts. But, in deciding on which software to purchase, looking at some of the specific features may be helpful. I have listed some features in order of importance and explained each briefly. Some may be more important to you than others. You will have to assess the kinds of word-processing applications that will be most important in your business. In the brand-name rating comments in the appendix, some of these features will be referred to in terms of advantages and disadvantages of specific systems.

General Editing. The main functions to look for are character, word, line, or paragraph insertion and deletion, using the fewest number of keystrokes. You also want to be able to switch easily from inserting new text to overtyping text that is already on the screen. Many programs have a "toggle" between the insert and overtype modes of editing.

Does the program require special codes for deleting,

inserting, or overtyping? How many keystrokes are required to insert a character or a word? Here you might want to test the program by seeing how quickly the person demonstrating it can move the cursor from the top of a paragraph to the end of the next paragraph. What are the options for deletion? Must it be done character by character or can you delete words, lines and paragraphs? How easy or difficult is it to do this? Also, since even experienced operators will make deletion errors, what protection, if any, is there for replacing accidental deletions? Ask to see how an accidentally deleted line or sentence can be "undeleted."

Block Operations. In any heavy word-processing application, the ability to move, copy, or delete blocks of text is important. This comes in handy, for example, when you want to switch around the order of two paragraphs or move a section of one document to another, leaving the first document intact. It is also helpful to have the ability to use a single or double keystroke to repeat some phrases, sentences, or blocks of material that recur in different places in your work. For instance, you may have a 75-word product description repeated several times throughout the document. If you can treat it as a block and recall it throughout the document when necessary, instead of retyping it, this will save time.

Ideally, you want to be able to identify the beginning and the end of the block. Then you want to have the option of moving it somewhere else in the document, deleting it, transferring it to a different document, or copying it somewhere else in the same document. Good word-processing programs allow easy identification of blocks and simple one- or two-keystroke block operation commands.

Printer Formatting. This refers to setting your printed output in terms of margins, vertical lines spacing, right versus left versus full justification and starting and stopping justification within a document. Since you will be producing a wide variety of documents, even small considerations in fiexibility are important. In a document, the printer often has to make a lot of changes on the same page. For example, the margins may change in the middle of the page for the indented paragraph, the justification may go on and off, and both boldface and underlining may be used. Not all word-processing programs will support all of these functions. Even if they do support these functions, the printer you are using is the ultimate determiner of whether or not these functions can actually be implemented on the job. However, since you may choose your printer after you select your software (or you may in the future decide to upgrade your printer), you should select the word-processing software that is most flexible in printer formatting and output options.

Repagination. Most word-processing applications will require automatic repagination since most jobs are more than one page in length. Virtually all the available word-processing software can break lengthy files into page-length sections, but the elegance and detail with which they do this varies widely. You want to be able to specify points at which a break should or should not take place. For example, (you may want a forced break at the end of a section or no break in the middle of a chart or a table. "Smart" word-processing programs automatically recognize "widow" and "orphan" lines – those lines that hang at the beginning or end of a paragraph and should not begin or end a new page.

When your file is repaginated, possibly several times over the course of draft revision, the pages should be automatically numbered in a format that is acceptable to you. You may want to number some documents on the top right, some in the top center, and some on the bottom of the page. Page numbering may be numeric characters (80, 81, etc.) or configured with characters, hyphens, periods, or some other punctuation (8-14, 8/15, 8.16, [8:17], etc.). You may want the first page of a document numbered on the bottom, but all subsequent pages numbered on the top. Especially important are what are called "headers" and "footers". These include the page numbers, the vertical spaces (or top and bottom page margins), and possibly a title or other designation automatically included with the pagination.

Columnar Word Processing. Working with multiple columns on a page, such as you find in tables or listings, poses special problems with many word-processing systems. It is often perplexing to a neophyte who tries to understand why a sophisticated computer cannot simply "understand" the idea of a column. But the answer is simple. Computers and their word-processing programs tend to be much more simple-minded and literal than human beings. They see all lines of text as running across the page from left to right, margin to margin. You can easily recognize that a two-column document or table should be read partly across and partly down. You can also see where one column ends and the next column begins. But these are challenges to a computer. Since you might be working with tables and columns, however, you should see how well your word-processing software handles this task. This feature is important in revising double-column work or updating statistical tables.

Special Features. The fierce competition among manufacturers of word-processing software packages for microcomputers has encouraged the development of many valuable features which are nearly standard in today's better-quality packages. *Find and replace* (also called *global search and replace*) is an important feature that allows you to search quickly through a long document and change a word or several words automatically. It also allows you to get quickly to a specified place in a file and stop there for additional commands or editing. For example, if you know that at some point in a lengthy document you cited a case (*Litt Industries vs. New York Tire Supplies*) but you don't remember where it was, you can give a command to zip through the document until that reference is found. This is also useful for locating and changing the spelling of a word that you discover was misspelled throughout the document (if you spelled Mr. Smyth as Mr. Smith, for example).

Spelling checker programs (also called dictionary programs) automatically proofread your documents for spelling errors and, based on their dictionaries, offer corrections for misspelled words. Some of these programs are now standard parts of many word-processing software packages or they may be sold separately as options that work in conjunction with a given program. Spellstar™ works in conjunction with Wordstar™, for example, and Perfect Speller™ is the dictionary program for the Perfect Writer™ word-processing program. Other programs that check and correct grammatical problems and usage questions are also becoming popular, although their value for word-processing applications is more tenuous.

Two other features are particularly useful for longer documents. The first is the ability to do automatic footnoting—to place the correct footnote at the bottom of the page on which its corresponding number appears. The second is the ability to create an index at the end of the document, or a table of contents at the beginning. Both are based on words or headings which have been "flagged" (usually with a @ or <) within the document.

Even more important than these conveniences, especially for the person who will be running his or her own word-processing business, is a mailing (also called *Mail Merge*) program, used for sending out mass mailings. This type of program may be a part of the word-processing package or may be sold separately. It allows you to generate and print letters by combining files of mailing lists with a standard letter. A good program will do this merging semi-automatically and will be able to insert variable material in the body of the letter as well as in the inside address.

Software Rating Comparison Chart

To help you evaluate and choose from the range of word-processing software, I have developed a rating chart which allows you to make a comparative assessment of different programs. It has been constructed to identify, assess, and give weighted values to those functions that are most important for long-range satisfaction with a word-processing system. You should note that two categories, generally considered important in magazine reviews about word-processing software, are omitted here: *ease of learning* and *error handling*. I am not especially concerned about the former since you have to learn a system only once. As I've mentioned before and will mention again, the easier a system is to learn, the more likely it is to be limited in use. Error handling is important but has been omitted here for a good reason. All the recommended, popular programs today have very good to excellent error handling (that is, they don't typically crash if you make a mistake). Moreover, since this quality is something you would probably not be able to evaluate through your own testing, it is not included in the ratings.

Using this rating system, you can compare the relative virtues of the word-processing software you are considering using for your business. Every "yes" answer counts as a plus one (+ 1) unless a higher value is indicated in parentheses, in which case it is judged important enough to count more (+ 2, + 3, etc.). The highest rating is 149, and several of the major programs will score this, and are of equal value. This means that your decision will be based on price, on vendor support, and on the availability of friends and colleagues to help you master the software. The subtotal for each main category is listed under the category title. Although some important features, such as cursor movement, are important in your daily operation, they are not weighted as heavily as features like page formatting and printer control. This is because they are assumed to perform with relative equality in all the popular word-processing programs.

CURSOR MOVEMENT   SUB-TOTAL (10)

(+2)	_____	use of direction arrows
(+1)	_____	by character
(+1)	_____	by word
(+1)	_____	by sentence
(+1)	_____	by line
(+1)	_____	by paragraph
(+1)	_____	by screen
(+1)	_____	by tab settings (fixed or defined)
(+1)	_____	to beginning and end of file

DELETING TEXT   SUB-TOTAL (10)

(+2)	_____	insert/delete toggle
(+1)	_____	single character
(+1)	_____	whole words
(+1)	_____	part lines (line end)
(+1)	_____	whole lines
(+1)	_____	whole sentence
(+1)	_____	whole paragraph
(+1)	_____	whole page
(+1)	_____	whole document

RECOVERING ACCIDENTAL DELETIONS
SUBTOTAL (10)

(+5)	_____	"undelete" or recover
(+5)	_____	blocks, pages, or entire files

SCROLLING   SUBTOTAL (10)

(+2)	_____	by line, fast or slow
(+1)	_____	by page
(+1)	_____	through entire document
(+5)	_____	backwards and forwards
(+1)	_____	split-screen scrolling

BLOCK OPERATIONS   SUBTOTAL (25)

	_____	ease of entering "block mode" to copy, delete or move text.
(+10)	_____	exceptionally easy
(+7)	_____	very easy
(+5)	_____	easy
(+3)	_____	somewhat difficult
(+0)	_____	difficult

SEARCH AND REPLACE   SUBTOTAL (13)

(+5)	_____	ease of toggling to search-/find/replace mode
(+5)	_____	ease or difficulty of identifying search/find/replace strings
(+2)	_____	global find and replace
(+1)	_____	user-confirmed find and replace breadth of search (document, page, etc.)

PAGE FORMATTING   SUBTOTAL (23)

(x15)	_____	headers and footers
(x1)	_____	with automatic page
(+1)	_____	numbering options
(+1)	_____	odd/even (recto/verso)
(+1)	_____	page distinctions
+	_____	page break controls
(+1)	_____	automatic paragraph indenting and spacing
(+1)	_____	hyphenation options
(+1)	_____	variable line spacing on page

PRINTER FORMAT AND CONTROL SUBTOTAL (22)

(+15)	_____	proportional/justified/variable
(+1)	_____	pitch
(+1)	_____	underline
(+2)	_____	bold face
(+1)	_____	superscripts/subscripts
(+1)	_____	continuous (page, document, file) printing option with/without pause
+1)	_____	on-screen previewing

SPECIAL FEATURES   SUBTOTAL (22)

(+20)	_____	ease of learning
(+1)	_____	glossary feature
+	_____	mailing list/file merging

These special features count even if they require an optional purchase.

SUBTOTAL (4)

(+1)	_____	word processing programming options
(+1)	_____	index, bibliography, references, footnote, support features
(+1)	_____	graphics capabilities
(+1)	_____	special hardware support, including telecommunications

TOTAL (149)

MAKING YOUR SELECTION

When I asked people to comment objectively on what they believed to be the best available word-processing program, they all recommended the one they were using. The following list contains the results of the eight interviews I conducted.

Applewriter (1)
EXECUTIVE SECRETARY (1)
Perfect Writer (2)
Select (1)
Word Star (3)

People who are using word-processing programs are so comfortable with their own that they cannot comment objectively about the other programs. In fact, I have discovered that even if shown an easier or more powerful program, most people will stay with an old program because they perceive the new one as more difficult.

I mention this to point out that you shouldn't always rely on the recommendation of someone who is currently using – and is happy with – done particular word-processing program. The objective rating chart on the preceding pages, reading reviews in popular computer magazines and a hands-on demonstration will help you choose the right word-processing software.

Based on dozens of interviews with people who use word-processing software regularly, and thousands of pages of reviews and documentation, I have put together a brief critique of some word-processing programs that can be recommended most highly. These are listed in Appendix B. Some programs might have an edge over others in certain areas, but no one of these is unequivocally better than the rest. You would be safe with any of them.

If you are in the process of making your decision now, look at the special pluses and minuses of the software to see if one is better matched to your needs than another. If you are buying a bundled machine (one that already comes with software) such as Morrow or Kaypro, then you will probably see your software on the list already.

3

Selecting the "Best" Word Processor For Your Business

The word processor you select will largely determine your investment in capital and time. The cost of a functioning word-processing system ranges today from $2500 to $18,000, with anticipated yearly maintenance and service from $200 to $1200. Operator pay ranges from $6.00 per hour to $15.00 per hour, depending largely on the operator employment pool. This pool varies from a surplus to a shortage of operators for different systems at different times, and in different geographical regions. The time it takes to train a good typist to become a word-processing operator ranges from 15 hours to 90 hours. You can see why the selection of the right system is a very important factor in your initial business decisions.

If you are reading this before you've made a purchase decision, then you will be focusing first on the critical question of whether to buy a *dedicated word processor* – that is, one built specifically for editing text, formatting and printing documents and letters—or to buy a microcomputer, with appropriate word-processing software.

If you already have some equipment, you might be asking how to best "configure" it. "Configure" means putting together the discrete parts of the system (more memory, communications, etc.) so that the system will function most effectively. Or, you may find as you read this chapter that there are software or hardware options on the market for your system that can significantly upgrade your computer to a powerful word processor with a minimal expense. Appendix B lists my recommendations of several excellent systems by their brand name. We are going to begin, however, by debating the merits of a dedicated system versus a microcomputer.

"DEDICATED" WORD PROCESSOR OR MICROCOMPUTER?

As you begin to think about your business plans, you are faced at the outset with the choice between a microcomputer and a dedicated word processor. Microcomputers are available under such popular brand names as Apple, TRS, the IBM-PC®, Digital's Rainbow-PC, Kaypro™, Victor, Morrow, Eagle, Compaq™, Texas Instruments, Columbia, Corona™, Hyperion, Franklin™, and North Star. The dedicated word processors, which are also made by IBM and Digital (the Displaywriter and the Decmate, respectively), are manufactured by companies like Wang, CPT, Exxon, Xerox, Micom and NBI. (NBI, incidentally, was founded by former IBM personnel. Those now-famous initials stand for, believe it or not, *N*othing *B*ut *I*nitials).

Many people in the computer field believe that there are no real distinctions between a microcomputer and a dedicated word processor. By now, they argue, all the so-called dedicated word processors are really just plain microcomputers which are marketed and designed somewhat differently. In older equipment the dedicated word processor was designed solely for text editing and printing while the microcomputer was designed as a true multipurpose computing and programming machine. This unequivocal distinction no longer exists. Today's machines are all more versatile and amenable to a range of tasks. But there are still several differences you should be aware of.

Probably the greatest single difference in today's equipment is in the way it is marketed or sold, which in turn affects the price. Microcomputers are sold widely through retail outlets, including department stores, stereo and electronic stores, and mail-order discount warehouses. Word processors, on the other hand, are sold primarily by the manufacturers, through their well-paid sales representatives. You may find some reconditioned units, marketed by private brokers. Microcomputers are usually directed toward the consumer market as well as toward businesses and professionals. Word processors, on the other hand, are sold exclusively to businesses and professionals. The person making a purchase decision, for either a microcomputer or word processor, will be bombarded with literature and sales pitches, and will probably become quite confused.

Although microcomputers are increasingly being used for heavy-load word-processing applications – in fact word processing is one of the three main uses of microcomputers – dedicated word processors still hold some advantages. A person whose primary application is writing, generating many letters, editing, or running a word processing business will make the best of a dedicated word processor. The microcomputer can serve many masters and offers the flexibility to run programs from games to graphics to graphological analysis. However, the word processor has been designed to excel at word-processing and text-editing applications from hardware through the documentation. It is the unrivaled expert in that dedicated task.

The word processor screen is designed to display at least 80-character-wide lines of text. Upper case and lower case letters as well as special characters, such as superscripts and underlines, are also featured. The cables and independent parts are all factory-connected and working at delivery. When you purchase a microcomputer and printer system you then have to figure out how to set it up. The word processor's editing and printing logic requires no compromises because it is one piece of equipment not used by the software designer and, therefore, not responsive to some of the program codes. This is a big problem with microcomputers. A writer might find that the word-processing software won't work properly with the printer that came with the special package, and now nothing can be printed in double spaces.

A dedicated word processor often includes special text editing keys (Page End, Line Out, Character Enter, Character Delete) for rapid access and editing. It also offers a degree of cursor responsiveness and speed not generally found in microcomputers. Moreover, because it is designed to be used for extensive amounts of typing, its keyboard has been especially configured for text editing applications. What might require many coded operations on a computer can be executed through a single keystroke on a dedicated word processor.

A big difference between these two types of hardware is price and support. Dedicated word processors usually cost about twice as much as a comparable microcomputer system. In addition, you may still have to pay several hundred dollars extra for the circuit board and software to give the dedicated word processor the versatility of a typical microcomputer, and allow it to run programs written for CP/M® or PC DOS® computers. On the plus side, since most dedicated word processors are sold by the manufacturers, you tend to get better technical support after installation. There are usually people who know how these things work and what you can do with your expensive piece of equipment. This is an advantage if your entire business depends on your word processor working properly, and on proficient operators.

Still, there is no simple rule to help you choose one over the other. It is always a trade-off. With the microcomputer, you get enormous versatility and expandability built into the base price. With the word processor, you get a nice balance of ease of use, word-processing power, and efficiency in operator time.

It is best to evaluate both dedicated word processors and microcomputers. Ultimately, your choice will boil down to a cost/benefit ratio. This is sometimes tricky to compute, especially when prices touted in ads (an Apple IIe® advertised on sale for an appealing $999) may be about one fourth of what it actually costs to set up a viable word-processing system. Prices quoted for dedicated word processors are generally complete, but microcomputer systems require the addition of several "peripherals" to get them functioning properly as word processors. An example of this kind of advertising ploy, very common in the industry, is given in Table 3.1, along with the actual cost.

You can see that the advertised cost of a microcomputer is often far below the actual cost of a working system. You should, in fact, expect to spend between three and six thousand dollars to get a running microcomputer-based word-processing system — one that is complete, efficient and produces letter-quality manuscript. Some of the ads you see in the paper are often nothing more than "bait and switch" lures. These ads may be designed to get you into the store so you can be sold a complete system at a much higher price than you originally planned to spend.

Reconditioned Word Processors

The alternative to buying a new microcomputer or new

Table 3.1

TRUE COSTS OF A
WORD PROCESSING SYSTEM

Advertisement Says

Brand A Computer
with connecting cables
Regular Price: $3,098
NOW ONLY $999
25 Free Programs - Glare Free Monitor

Actual Cost

Advertised Special. $999
Two Disk Drives with controller. $800
Letter Quality Printer. $2,000
Word Processing Software. $399
                                                    Total $4198

Alternative

Reconditioned
  • Vydec
  • Xerox
  • IBM
  • Lanier
word processor-complete   Approx. $4300.00

word processor (usually over $7,000) is to purchase a recon-
ditioned word-processing system. This option is especially
attractive since such units typically come with guarantees
of eligibility for *manufacturer's service* contract (also called a
maintenance agreement). This means the vendor is assuring
you (*be sure it is in writing*) that the manufacturer of the
equipment will sell you a service contract. Such assurance
is basically equivalent to the guarantee on a new unit, since
your service contract will cover all aspects of the unit's
functioning and provide free replacement parts.

Be sure to check the cost of servicing the equipment; it
is typically between $900 and $1,500 per year. This may
seem expensive, but it is absolutely necessary to protect
against sudden, large maintenance expenses. If a printer
has to be replaced, for example, it could cost several thousand dollars. Labor costs are typically over $70 an hour for
manufacturer's technicians. Moreover, regular servicing,
which is part of your maintenance agreement, can help to
extend the life of your equipment to well over 10 years.

The best way to find a reconditioned unit is by a recommendation from someone who has bought a unit from a
second-hand dealer. You can also find advertisements in
many leading business- and computer-related magazines.
Dealers are sometimes listed in the *Business-to-Business
Yellow Pages,* under "Word Processors – Dealers."

There are three things to consider when purchasing a
reconditioned unit. First, and foremost, be sure the unit is
either currently covered by a service contract, or that you
have a written guarantee, preferrably *from the manufacturer*, that it qualifies for a manufacturer's service contract.
This means that the machine will, for a stipulated annual
fee, be protected against small and large breakdowns. A
factory-trained field engineer will repair or replace – at the
manufacturer's expense – parts that burn out, wear out or
break down.

A service contract, in this request, is like a general

health insurance policy. It not only takes care of unantici-
pated major catastrophes that are hideously expensive to fix
(a burned-out CRT can cost $700.00 to replace), but also
takes care of the small, everyday problems and maintenance that will keep the machine in good repair. Moreover,
a service contract generally assures a quick response to
service calls. If your machine is down, you don't want to
wait several days to have it repaired. Most companies guarantee same-day response to calls for downed equipment.
There is a caveat: don't accept a guarantee of servicability
from the seller. It is virtually useless. If a machine is really
in good condition, the manufacturer's servicing department
will issue a service contract.

Also, if you are planning to have an operator work the
machine, make sure there is a supply of trained operators
available. Many of the machines that appeared on the market during the mid 1970s disappeared from the market so
quickly that a sufficient number of people were never
trained to operate them. If you have to train all your operators, it will be expensive in terms of time and personnel
problems.

Finally, be sure that the person or firm from whom you
are buying the reconditioned word processor actually owns
it. Stories are legion of individuals who jumped at a chance
to own their own word processors only to find out six
months later that the machines they just purchased were
part of an unfulfilled lease agreement. They didn't own
even a slice of them. This situation can be avoided by asking
an attorney to look over the purchase agreement and to
evaluate the seller's proof of ownership claim.

MAKING YOUR DECISION

As you evaluate your options, you will want to consider, separately, the hardware, the software, and special
features and options that can make your word processor

perform jobs that will save you time. The preceding chapter looked closely at how the word processor performs these time-saving jobs. It also looked closely at the word-processing software – the heart of any system. In the following discussion, the evaluation of each hardware and purchase-selection category is specifically tailored for individuals who are running a word-processing business or are heavily dependent upon their word processors.

The major criteria of my evaluation are the abilities to generate, edit, and print short, medium-length, and long documents (over 20 pages); the ability to format and print hundreds of form letters; reliability and serviceability. Other popular features of microcomputers, such as video graphics, budget forecasting, home thermostat control, and so on, are irrelevant to word processing and are not given consideration here. That is why I do not mention Commodore, Coleco, or Atari computers. All are popular computers that are not suitable to heavy-duty word-processing applications. If you are planning to use your computer not only for word processing, but for many different functions, you will want to take this into account as you read the following.

Keyboard. The standard typewriter keyboard that comes with the computer is called a QWERTY keyboard, named after the six leftmost keys above the home row (the row you keep your fingers on). It was designed in the late nineteenth century by Christopher Shoals as a method of slowing down typists who were typing so fast that the keybars constantly jammed. (Because of the lack of precision tooling and stamping machinery at that time, the type bars – the mechanical parts that strike the ribbon to imprint letters on the paper – would often jam). Shoals discovered the order of keys that would be most difficult on which to speed type and patented it. He placed the keys commonly struck in a sequence far from each other. The e and i, the q and u, the a and l are far apart in this configuration. Iron-ically, when today's word processors can process thousands of characters per second, we are still using a keyboard designed one hundred years ago to slow us down.

There is an alternative to the deliberately slow QWERTY configuration, called the Dvorak Keyboard. The Dvorak keyboard places the most commonly used letters on the middle row, so the typists' fingers rarely have to move. Typing strain (measured in distance traveled by the fingers) is reduced about six times with the Dvorak keyboard and typing speed is about doubled. The disadvantage is that typists who are used to QWERTY have a difficult time adjusting to Dvorak. However, if you don't already type, and you want to learn, the Dvorak keyboard may be for you. It is available with Apple and DEC computers and as an add on for several others.

It is best if the keyboard is separate from the rest of the unit. This is called a detached keyboard, and it is connected by a cable to the computer. The advantage is that the oper-ator can position the keys in the most comfortable position and they can be moved as glare and other environmental conditions change. A combination keyboard and monitor or keyboard and central processing unit (CPU) generally lacks the flexibility of a separate keyboard. The normal typing keyboard has about 53 keys, but most computer and word processing keyboards have 70-100, many of them cursor control and editing keys. More is not necessarily better. Some things to consider in evaluating the keyboard in order of importance are:

- how the keyboard feels to the touch, (don't judge this at once; even a good keyboard will feel uncomfortable at first if you are used to an inferior one)
- if the keyboard displays special characters and codes;
- if editing function keys are easily readable and conven-iently located

- if you do a lot of number entry input, you should evaluate the numeric pad (the number keys you find on a calculator). This factor is unnecessary if you don't do much calculation as it may just add weight and space to the keyboard.

Monitor. The quality of a monitor screen, sometimes called the display, is extremely important for word-processing applications, since you will be staring at it for hours on end. For word processing, a monochromatic monitor, featuring white, green, or amber letters on a black background is preferable (Figure 3.1). Colored monitors are unsuitable for word processing because they cannot produce clear characters. You will want to see clear, delineated letters, regardless of how many characters you display on a line or have on the screen.

Many monitors, perfectly satisfactory for data processing input or video game applications, are unsuitable for the demands of word processing. Some things to consider are: can the monitor generate both uppercase and lowercase characters clearly? Can it tilt or swivel for viewer comfort? Are the monitor's color and resolution (clarity) good for long-term viewing? (Inputting and editing require significantly more monitor exposure than data processing does and the operator should be able to control the screen's brightness level.) Does the monitor allow enough lines to be displayed? Does it allow the full line width of the word-processing software's capabilities? Most monitors allow 80 characters of text per line and feature 24 or more lines of viewing. The number of dots that make up characters vary, but the more dots the better. Some monitors are capable of wide-screen viewing, with as many as 132 characters per line. This might be an advantage for some word-processing applications.

Courtesy of NEC Home Electronics (U.S.A.), Inc.

Figure 3.1 A computer monitor looks much like an ordinary TV, but offers considerably better resolution and clarity.

Storage Device. There are two main kinds of magnetic storage media suitable for word-processing applications: floppy disks (also called diskettes or flexible disks) and hard disks.

Some microcomputers will work with tape cassette systems. While this is fine for some applications, it is not adequate for word processing for two reasons. First, tape is very slow in getting or retrieving information. Second, a tape always has to be played in sequence; for example, to get to the third page you have to first go through pages one and two. Also, if you want to add a long block to page three, the entire tape has to be reformatted. Each time you add material, the tape gets longer, making the entire process quite cumbersome and suitable only for short documents, such as letters.

For all intents and purposes, floppy disks are suitable for heavy-duty word processing and most office management applications. For an effective word-processing system, you will need two 5 1/4-inch or 8-inch disk drives. Neither size is better, how much information can be stored on a disk, is what ultimately counts. Disk drives and floppy disks are described as being one of the following:

SINGLE SIDED, SINGLE DENSITY, SOFT SECTORED

SINGLE SIDED, SINGLE DENSITY, HARD SECTORED

DOUBLE SIDED, DOUBLE DENSITY, SOFT SECTORED

DOUBLE SIDED, SINGLE DENSITY, HARD SECTORED

DOUBLE SIDED, QUAD DENSITY, SOFT SECTORED

SINGLE SIDED, QUAD DENSITY, SOFT SECTORED

These terms describe whether information is stored on one or both sides of the disk (single or double sided), how compactly it is stored (single or double density), and whether the storage areas are determined by software or predetermined by index holes in the disk (hard sectoring). But the terms don't really matter very much since there is another way of evaluating the efficacy of your disk drive. It is simply this: the more information that can be stored on a disk, the better.

Information is measured in bytes, a thousand of which are called a kilobyte, commonly abbreviated K. Most systems hold between 10K and 500K per disk. Since your word-processing program will be on one disk, and may be required to stay in the disk drive during operation, it is almost always necessary to have two disk drives. The exception is when the program is "hardwired" into the equipment – as with a dedicated word processor – and all disk space is available for storage. Then you can get away with one disk drive. When you purchase a system, you should find out how many Ks of data its disk can hold. A general rule is that double-sided storage is more economical than single-sided, but in the end, only the number of kilobytes really counts.

Recently there has been a growing trend to use hard disks in microcomputer systems. Unlike a floppy disk, the hard disk is made of aluminum and coated with a magnetic material. It is housed in a protective cartridge which isolates it from the elements. The read/write head in the disk drive does not touch the surface of a hard disk, as it does a floppy, but instead floats slightly above the disk surface.

The great attraction of the hard disk is its tremendous storage capacity. Hard disk storage is measured in millions of bytes (megabytes), not thousands. While a floppy disk may hold 500K, a good hard disk system can hold five to twenty megabytes (millions of bytes) – thousands of pages of information at one time. If you are typing a doctoral dissertation, for example, or a book-length project, you can literally have the entire manuscript at your fingertips at any given moment simply by issuing a disk command. Also, you can get information on or from a hard disk much more quickly than with a floppy disk. This allows you to transfer text to and from memory at a more productive rate. But the hard disk has its disadvantages, too. It is much more expensive than a floppy disk system. The hard disk is also rather sensitive to things like dust particles and cigarette smoke, which can cause serious disk failure. Recently, however, better-designed, protective air-sealed cartridges have been developed to mitigate this problem. Modern hard disk drives can add immensely to the value and utility of your word-processing system.

The Printer. The most important question here is, how good is the print quality? When you are in the word-processing business, you have to be able to generate typed output that boasts uncompromising quality.

There are four main kinds of printers: IBM-element types (the ubiguitous "golf ball" element); daisy wheel printers (with plastic or metal flat print wheels having 96 spokes – each with a different character); dot-matrix printers (characters made from small dots); and ink-jet printers (characters formed by spraying ink on the paper).

In addition to the print quality, there are several other important considerations. How fast does it print? This will be especially important as your word-processing business starts to grow. You will find that your single largest expense will be operator salaries. It is not difficult to imagine how frustrating it will be to see your operator sitting while the printer prints a page of text in two minutes, while another printer could do the same job in 40 seconds.

Generally, the faster a printer prints, the more expensive it is and the more prone it is to break down; but this is not always so. Speed, translated into output, means that on an average manuscript page, double spaced, with pica size type, it will take 100 seconds to print at 15 cps and 38 seconds at 40 cps. Considering the time it takes to insert the paper, line it up, and then remove it at the end of printing, the printer speed is not the only thing to consider in timing. An operator's speed in paper insertion and removal can vary as much as 200%, outweighing any advantages built into the printer.

In addition to print quality and speed, the question of versatility is important. Will your printer allow you to change type styles? Is the process simple or complex? Can the pitch (10 pitch "pica" or 12 pitch "elite") be changed? Can it print graphs and other graphic-type materials? Does it underline and print bold face? Can it output foreign-lan-

Courtesy of Centronics, Inc.

Figure 3.2 An automatic sheet feeder can save a substantial amount of operator time during large printing jobs.

guage characters and special science symbols? All these things are important in the professional word-processing business and have to be weighed in making your decision.

Finally, the questions of reliability and maintenance expenses have to be taken into consideration. Where will your printer be serviced when it breaks down? Notice, I say *when* rather than *if,* since printers break down more frequently than any other part of the word-processing system.

How much does a maintenance contract cost and what guarantee of speedy repairs is offered? Are parts available in my geographical area?

Evaluation of Types of Printers

The IBM selectric element-type printers are outdated. They are very slow (about 17 cps) and highly prone to breakdowns in word-processing applications (which is not their fault since they were never designed for high-speed printing). However, they do offer excellent print quality and versatility). To change type styles, you simply remove the element and replace it with any one of a score of others available. These include international character sets and a variety of mathematical and scientific characters. But the disadvantages far outweigh the advantages and these printers cannot be recommended.

Some firms, especially those that advertise in small computer magazines, are pushing reconditioned selectric typewriters as printers for microcomputer word-processing applications. But these machines were never designed for heavy-duty output and their performance record has been less than satisfactory. They should be avoided.

The daisy wheel printers offer letter-quality printing as good as that of the finest electric typewriter, with great versatility, good reliability, and decent speed. This type of printer spins a 4-inch diameter, spoked print wheel, with molded plastic, metal, or fiberglass characters at the end of each spoke. As the appropriate letter reaches the top position, lined up with the printing hammer, the hammer strikes it. This causes the character to hit the ribbon and leave its imprint on the paper. Daisy wheel printers vary in speed from about 12cps to 55cps. The faster they are, as you might expect, the more expensive they are. The print wheel can be easily changed and the variety of character sets available is about the same as the element-types. Daisy wheel printers, like element printers, cannot accommodate graphics capabilities, since they are limited to the character set on their element or wheel.

The dot-matrix impact printer has become an increasingly attractive alternative for many individuals who are considering purchasing a word processor. But it has its limitations for professional word processing applications.

A matrix printer (also called an impact dot-matrix printer) has a single print head made up of tiny pins that form a matrix, or grid. Patterns of these pins (in the form of characters or special symbols) strike the ribbon and leave an impression on the paper. The number of pins used ranges from a general low of 5x7 (or 35 squares to the grid) to a more typical 7x9 (or 63 squares). Some manufacturers are using staggered pin wires in the head to create more solid-looking letters on impact. Many dot-matrix printers also have enhanced printing modes. This means that the head strikes over each letter twice or more, either darkening it, filling it in, or making the letter wider or larger. On the Epson MX-80 or Okidata 92, for instance, you can double the width of characters, strike over characters twice, or compress letters. Some software will enable you to control these functions, but some will not. In most cases, however, before you load the word-processing software into the system you can give commands directly to the printer to print in its special capabilities.

This is sometimes referred to as high-density printing. Because the pins are controlled by the software, they can print in a great number of defined configurations. These include letters and numerals of different types styles, lines and graphics, and as many special, user-defined characters as are needed. The matrix printer is capable, sometimes with a circuit board option added, of a far greater range of output than can be provided by the 96 spokes of the print wheel. It is also much faster: generally from 80 to 200 characters per second.

The big disadvantage of the dot-matrix unit is the print quality. The earlier models, which produced the hazy letters which we associate with low-quality matrix printing, were totally unacceptable for manuscript and letter output. Today, many matrix printers use multiple-pass printing, in which the printhead passes over the line more than once, producing much better output. Some of this output is so good that it can almost pass for daisy wheel output – but not quite. Although pages printed by a dot matrix are not of the quality of those printed by a daisy wheel, some firms now accept them. They usually would not expect to get them from a professional word-processing operation, however. You might consider purchasing both a dot-matrix printer and a daisy wheel printer. This may seem expensive, but it pays off in the long run. The dot-matrix unit can print drafts of the final copy for your client to proofread and correct much more quickly than the daisy wheel unit. This increases your total productivity significantly. And if you also own a daisy wheel, you can still offer state-of-the-art print quality in the final output.

When making a purchase decision about a printer, you will invariably come across the terms "correspondence-quality" and "letter-quality" output. Correspondence-quality generally means that the dot-matrix printer outputs a quality that is considered suitable for most correspondence (letters, memos, etc.). Letter-quality means that the printhead, by making multiple passes, can output characters close to daisy wheel specifications. However, there are no clear industry standards about what constitutes letter-quality or correspondence-quality. The best idea is to have a live demonstration of the machine's output, using the same word-processing software you intend to use. Also, be aware that these enhanced print modes are significantly slower than the single-pass, draft quality printing. You may end up with a dot-matrix printer that produces less than daisy wheel quality at less than daisy wheel speed.

The ink-jet printer has been hailed as the perfect cross between daisy wheel output quality and matrix printing speed. Using a small cartridge of special ink, much like a little paint spray can, this remarkable type of printer shoots the ink through an electrostatic grid to form the letters on paper. It is fast – about 100 cps or more – and the quality is excellent. The problems are the prices and the reliability. Fast ink-jet printers are very expensive and there are not many trained service technicians who can repair them. Since the ink dries on the paper, you must also use a decent quality paper, even for draft printing. Also, you cannot make carbon copies with an ink jet. However, theoretically, it is so fast that you can print another original faster than an impact printer can print one copy.

Printer Enhancements

As I mentioned earlier, the speed of the printer is not always the single most critical factor in how long it takes to get your printing done. The time it takes for an operator to insert envelopes and sheets of paper, line them up and remove them, all add significantly to the total printing time. In fact, running two hundred short letters and envelopes may require more insertion and removal time than it does actual printing time.

Two printer attachments, the automatic sheet feeder and automatic envelope feeder, are designed to solve this problem. As their names imply, they automatically send the sheet of paper or envelope into the printer, line it up, and eject it when it is fully printed. The operator can print a 60-page document during a lunch break by setting the right commands, and loading the paper. Sounds great? Well, it is to a degree; but the drawbacks are great, too.

Automatic envelope and sheet feeders are very expensive – typically, well over a thousand dollars. They are prone to mishap, especially jamming, and require a lot of maintenance. More importantly, they must work in conjunction with your printer *and* software. You have to be sure of the correct combination – a rare and fortuitous streak of luck. Your word-processing software must be capable of communicating to the printer and sheet feeder such commands as rolling the paper in and out, automatically setting up the next page, and changing margins as needed. Good luck!

A good compromise might be a forms tractor which accepts the standard-size, perforated, sprocket-hole paper. The paper is held in place and glided through by sprockets. Perforations allow you to separate it into single sheets and remove the sprocket tracks from the sides. This is a reliable and inexpensive alternative to a sheet feeder. However, you probably would not want to output all your final copy on this type of paper. A fussy customer might complain about the perforation lines. Recent advances in sprocket paper production have led to a technique called microperforation, in which the perforation bumps are almost invisible after removing the stubs and separating the sheets. Still, not all kinds of paper are available in this format, so you will be switching regularly between the tractor feed and the friction feed of the platen (the roller on which the paper rests).

Buffers and Spoolers

Other printer enhancements which are less expensive and well worth considering are buffers and spoolers (Figure 3.3). After the initial input typing has been completed, the printer is the slowest link in the word-processing chain. (This is true even of fast dot-matrix or ink jet printers.) So, when computing the time it takes you to do a complete job, your printer will be a major factor. One of the things that slows down many word-processing operations is waiting

Courtesy of Consolink Corporation

Figure 3.3 A print spooler, which takes very little desk room, can save you up to 60% in printing time by allowing the computer to be free while the printer is working. The model above can hold 16 pages of text while the printer is working.

for the printer to print one page before beginning your input typing or editing of the next page. In effect, because the printer is reading characters very slowly (15-200 characters per second) from your computer's memory, the computer and the operator are put on stand-by until the printing is finished.

This problem can be eliminated by using a *spooler* or *print buffer*. This hardware device serves as a temporary memory, holding information while the printer is printing, allowing the computer memory to be free for the next task.

By the way, there are software programs called *spooler programs* that attempt to do the same thing without hardware. However, they are far inferior to those that use an external hardware print buffer.

The buffer works very simply. When you give the print command to the printer, instead of the text being sent directly to the printer slowly, character by character, the whole batch is dumped into the buffer memory very quickly. The information then trickles to the printer at a speed the printer can handle. Your computer or word processor is immediately ready for its next task. This allows you to type or edit your next page while the printer is working on the first ones.

The buffers memory size determines how much it can hold at a time. Each single-spaced page is approximately 3000 characters (including codes for margins, justification, etc). So you would want at least 48K in your buffer to send through a 16 page report. Since a 16 page report takes about 15 minutes to type, you will be able to input at least two pages in the time it is printing. A pretty good savings, isn't it?

Buffers come in two basic forms: stand-alones or boards. The stand-alone is a piece of hardware that hooks up between the computer and the printer. The board accomplishes its spooling function inside the computer or the printer, housed in one of the peripheral slots. Stand-alones are suitable for almost all machines while boards, naturally, are designed for specific machines, such as the Apple or IBM computer, the NEC or Epson printer. A big advantage of a stand-alone, then, is that it can be used with another machine if you decide to upgrade in the future.

Recently, a number of software buffers have also been introduced. These are programs that partition an area of the computer's memory as a buffer. This area is then set aside until you give the print command, at which time the material to be printed is sent to the buffer. While the rest of the memory remains immediately available, this type of software does reduce your memory capacity significantly. It is only advantageous with a computer of 128K or more.

There are several features you will want to consider in selecting a buffer. These conveniences distinguish one 48K or 64K buffer from another, but some of them can add significantly to the cost. They may be hardwired into the circuits of the machine or they may rely on software that comes with the buffer.

The ability to "reset" and "clear" in midstream is important, especially if you decide to abort the printing operation in the middle of a document. The buffer's ability to receive data quickly from the computer is important. This is especially true if your computer is capable of sending data to the buffer at a rate of 19,200 bps (bits per second). The buffer, ideally, should accept it at the rate the computer sends it, and then drip it slowly to the printer at the rate the printer can accept it. The buffer should also be able to convert special telecommunication codes so that you can transmit data over phone lines or to other printers—and from other computers to your printer. You may also want the buffer to be able to print multiple copies of the same document. Some have what they call data compression capabilities that allow them to hold more data than their rated capacities. You may also want a buffer with LEDs (light emitting diodes) to show you what it is doing at a given time.

DOCUMENTATION AND SUPPORT

The legion of horror stories in this category no longer raise an eyebrow. The proud owner of the new computer gets it home, unpacks it, and loads the word-processing software. He carefully follows all the instructions, types a few sentences and when he goes to print, all he gets is nonsense. PHGS DFHOF DSH UDFSER WHOIFS!! He calls the friendly computer store and they tell him to call the software manufacturer. This manufacturer tells him there must be an error in the printer memory circuit; he should get in touch with the printer manufacturer. He gets in touch with the printer manufacturer who tells him to see the dealer who sold him the wrong printer for his system. And so it goes.

Because of this possible scenario, two of the most important criteria for choosing one system over another are the support given by the dealer and the quality of the system's documentation. By documentation, I mean the written instruction on how to operate the system and run the software. Generally, manufacturers of dedicated word-processing equipment offer excellent documentation and support. That service is built into their comparatively hefty price tag. Most dedicated word-processing vendors maintain a staff of trained, customer support representatives, thoroughly familiar with the equipment, whose sole job it is to assist purchasers *after* the delivery of their systems. The answer to your problem, if you've purchased a dedicated word processor from the manufacturer, is usually only a phone call away.

Mail order houses, which advertise regularly in computer magazines, generally give the least support, and sometimes none at all. Since you can't very well argue with them by mail, and long distance calls are expensive, you are basically out of luck. But this service disadvantage is reflected in the cost advantage of their very low prices, expecially for software. You can save anywhere from 15% to a full 60% in purchasing your software, and in many cases, your peripheral hardware, by mail or by toll-free phone. But don't expect any backup support if you have problems – and you will probably have some!

A reputable and knowledgeable salesperson in a computer store or a dealer in reconditioned word processors is, in the long run, your best bet. This vendor will charge for his or her service, but it is well worth the price. You will get information and support along with the equipment. Also, the person is located where you can go back, recommend friends, or cause a ruckus if you are unsatisfied or if the configuration fails to work as promised.

DON'T OVERBUY

Most people considering a word-processing system rely heavily on the promotions of the sales representatives, with good reason. These technically-knowledgeable people, trained by the manufacturer, are proud of what their systems can do and communicate their sense of enthusiasm to the prospective purchaser. The questions, however, that are most important to consider, especially for the purchaser on a budget, are: do I need all these functions and are they really as useful as stated?

For example, one of the most important selling features of word processors in recent years is the so-called dictionary feature. This capability, which relies on high-speed processing and a large memory, enables the computer to "proofread" a document in seconds and indicate misspelled words. This sounds great, bat at want be able two tell you that this sentiments makes know scents. My point is, the computer will read past the preceding sentence with approval because it doesn't understand what it is reading. Each individual word in that nonsense sentence (bat, at, want . . .) is in the dictionary, and therefore checks out. One ironic possibility to consider is this: if this feature is used extensively and writers come to rely on it, will they stop proofreading altogether? There might ultimately be *more* typographical errors with the use of this feature.

A feature typically promoted by the sales rep is the system's speed. Every machine is supposedly faster than the other. What the sales representative does not tell you is what we emphasized earlier; namely, that the weakest link in the chain is still the printer. Unless you are willing to spend a large amount for an ink jet printer, the output speed is not increased by faster processors, for which you may pay considerably more. So this touted feature is of interest chiefly to the technically-oriented.

The salesperson will tell you about unattended printing and automatic sheet or envelope feeders. These, however, are still in the process of proving themselves. Until you find out about one that is working effectively at a word-processing facility, you should not leave your word processor unattended for any length of time.

Another loudly touted feature is the 16-bit word processor. Many salespeople will point out that one machine is more expensive than the other since it is a 16-bit computer rather than a mere 8-bit. And, since 16 sounds much better than 8 – after all, it is twice as much – people are often willing to spend more for a 16-bit word processor.

But what does this specification actually mean? A bit is generally expressed as a 1 or 0, referring to an open or closed switch. Computers work by translating everything into these bits, so that the letter "Q" to the computer will look like this:

$$10101001$$

Likewise, the memory of a computer is made up of bits, including the instructions on how to process the information put into it.

Bits are grouped together into "bytes" or "words," the basic vocabulary of the computer. On an 8-bit computer each word is made up of a combination of ones or zeros. On a 16-bit computer, each word is made up of 16 ones and zeros. This difference affects the amount of memory available in the 8-bit and 16-bit machines. Theoretically, an 8-bit system has the capability of only 65,536 bytes of memory.

On the other hand, since there are more combinations of 1s and 0s in a 16-bit machine, its memory capability is considerably larger.

Despite this, there is no compelling reason to purchase a 16-bit computer over an 8-bit – especially for word-processing applications. First, 64K is sufficient for almost all word-processing capabilities. Even if it is not, there are machines on the market today that allow more than 64K, with 8-bit words. How do they do this? They use a technique called *bank switching*. This method uses several different memory banks to which information is added to and retrieved from by commands from the software. This makes it possible to have 8-bit machines with 128K memory or even more.

It is true, that 16-bit is important for very fast applications (real-time processing) and for very large, complex programs with lots of data (large accounting, payroll or spreadsheet programs). But at this time there is no evidence that 16-bit word processing has even the slightest advantage over 8-bit.

At present, the 16-bit argument is mainly a hype used by computer salespeople. For instance, you may be told the IBM is great because it's a 16-bit machine, but in many ways it is really like an 8-bit machine, since almost all of the popular IBM word-processing software is simply rewritten 8-bit software.

THE FINAL TEST: PUTTING IT ALL TOGETHER

In this and the preceding chapter, you have been shown the best and worst features of a typical word-processing system, and have been given a description of what a good word-processing system *should* do. When you go out to purchase your system, or to buy new software to upgrade your present one, it is imperative that you see a live demonstration of the system. First, allow the salesperson to show the suggested system (including the *exact* hardware and software combination you are considering buying). Take note of specific applications that impress you and the features that may be especially important for the specific kinds of word-processing business applications you anticipate. But never commit yourself to a system until you have seen a demonstration of its capabilities on a task that you present, not one suggested by the salesperson.

This caveat is important for three reasons. First, it helps you locate the weak points of a system. Naturally, each system has its limitations, either in the hardware, the software, or both. These limitations will not be highlighted in a demonstration by the dealer. It is your job as the intelligent consumer to figure out the soft spots before you get the system home.

Second, every system reflects some compromises in design and implementation. Many small functions and conveniences, not generally considered important, may be shelved during development in favor of more universally necessary and marketable functions. But since *your* business will reflect *your* specialized needs, you have to be sure that your specific applications can be fully handled by the system. For instance, WORDSTAR™ is generally acknowledged as one of the finest word-processing programs ever designed. It is indeed excellent for virtually all word-processing applications. But let us say that much of your specific business depends on producing camera-ready, proportionally-spaced, justified text for a company's newsletter. You have a DIABLO™ printer which can print this kind of output. This means that ideally, on the printed page the M should occupy more space than the narrower I. WORDSTAR cannot do this type of proportional spacing well. Therefore, although it is an excellent system, it might not be the best for your specific needs. GUTENBERG™, a less popular but equally powerful system allows proportional spacing and might be the one you would finally choose.

Finally, you are responsible for determining if the parts of your system will work together as a whole. Remember, unless you buy a dedicated word-processing system, you are purchasing a group of components that have not been specifically designed to work well with each other. Each attempts to be as universal as possible and this often requires trade-offs. Likewise, features of one part of the system may not be supported by another part. The word-processing software may be capable of justifying your printed output, but not with the printer you are buying. Or, the computer may be able to function quickly, but the software may be very slow in repagination or in input typing. Only through a live, hands-on demonstration that reflects the specific requirements of your business can you see how well or poorly these components work together.

The Benchmark Test

I suggest that you use a test like the one on the following pages to evaluate the overall performance, ease of use, and versatility of any system. Then design your own additional test to evaluate how well the system performs to your requirements. It's worth the extra time to avoid aggravation later on. Ask to input, edit and print this test by yourself, with the salesperson there to help you. That way you will see how easy or difficult it is to do – or whether the system is capable of it all.

I suggest, as the first page, a letter that challenges the system with a number of different tests (see Figure 3.4). How well does it handle two-level indenting, superscripts underlining, boldface, and the insertion of inside addresses text? Ask to see the word processor construct and print three letters to different addresses to see if the mailing list

March 7, 1984

Mr. Harrison Benchly, Esq.
PAULUS, SOLBY and GRILL
2984 West Brooklyn Ridge Rd.
Mainline, Mass. 02987

Dear Mr. Benchly:

Regarding our recent discussion concerning the efforts of your client, SAVANNAH INDUSTRIES, INC. to assume majority control of the stock and exercise managerial control over the day-to-day operations of our client, UNITED JERSEY BUS LINES, LTD., I want to reiterate the following points:

1. Our client has been in the public transportation field for 25 years with a record of <u>service</u> virtually unparalleled.

2. Previous takeover attempts have been thwarted[1] -- as <u>I am certain</u> this one will be, and that should be a consideration.

3. The rank-and-file[2] of UNITED JERSEY BUS LINES has, on two separate occasions, stated its opposition to this takeover move.

In response to your questions about our operating revenue and expenses, the figures on the enclosed schedule are, I believe, correct.

Sincerely,

Roger Winsome,
Attorney-at-law

cc; Bill Heart

---

[1] Including its parent company, NORTH SHORE RAPID TRANSIT.

[2] At the union meeting of December 19, 1983.

Figure 3.4 Test letter

and other information can be automatically inserted and printed. Then ask to edit the material, so you can evaluate the general editing and block-moving capabilities.

The next test uses columnar material and requires printing a document that is wider than the 80-character width of the screen (see Figure 3.5). These features are especially common in annual reports and statistical/accounting word processing. Also, ask if it is possible to move columns rather than having to retype them. Granted, this is generally a difficult task, but it brings together the functions of the software, printer, and monitor as few other tests can.

```
       NORTH SHORE RAPID TRANSIT   --- STATEMENT PREPARED   January 1984


                                                    1981         1982         1983


Revenues:
    Direct finance leasing--United States        $ 47,934    $ 45,932    $  45,039
    Direct finance leasing--Canada                             10,685       20,327
    Automotive fleet leasing                        46,426      35,110       21,139
    Operating lease programs                        43,480      20,096       13,117
    Lease financing programs                         9,834       8,572        6,638
    Equity in pretax earnings of Home Savings
        Association                                  3,645
    Equity in net income of associated foreign
        leasing companies                            1,543       3,097        3,659
    Sale of subsidiary and affiliates                           10,321
    ------------------------------------------------------------------------------
        Total revenues                             152,862     133,813      109,919
    ------------------------------------------------------------------------------
```

Figure 3.5 Test Columnar Report

4

The Start-Up Process

Once you have selected the best software and hardware for your word-processing business, you will have to realistically evaluate the demands your new business will make on you. You must assess *your* capabilities for meeting these demands before you can start your business on its way to success. You must begin to think as a business person, facing and overcoming a myriad of problems and making dozens of day-to-day decisions about how to build up your business. You will need a lot of practical information from others to save you the grief of having to learn from your own bad experiences. This chapter looks in detail at the starting up process. We begin by focusing on some of the questions and issues that challenge you from the outset. Although certain rules are cited from time to time, keep in mind that for every rule there are dozens of exceptions. Your particular situation may make you an exception.

HOME OR OFFICE?

The first question that you will have to ask is: can I run my business from home or do I have to rent office space? The advantages of running your business from home are threefold: (1) You save commuting time and can be very flexible with your hours; (2) you save office expenses; and (3) you can, if you use part of your home or apartment exclusively for work, deduct the cost of the space and the utilities from your taxes. This is all well and good, but there are also three disadvantages to consider on the other side: (1) your privacy (and that of your family or roommate) will be continually disturbed as clients come and go; (2) your home or apartment may not be zoned (or insured) for commercial enterprise and neighbors, landlords, or complaining customers may bring this to the attention of officials who can force you to close down; and (3) many clients respond less enthusiastically to the professionalism of people working from home than they do from those who work out of an office.

The pros and cons balance out, as you can see, and your final decision might be based on factors specific to your situation. For instance, some of the minuses might not apply to you:

- if you don't mind people coming to your house and no one else will be disturbed.
- if your apartment or home is zoned for light commerce.
- if you are able to get an insurance rider to cover your equipment.
- if you already have cheap or free commercial space available and it won't entail another expense.

Once you make your choice, you should keep in mind the suggestions in the following pages.

Working from Home

If you have decided to work from your home, you have a few things to do. First, you should have a telephone, separate from your regular home telephone, installed. This prevents the problem of having potential clients receive busy signals while you are talking to Aunt Lil. Such a problem can seriously cut down your business prospects because most clients are reluctant to keep dialing and will find someone else. Also, by having a phone dedicated to your business, you can deduct the cost from your taxes without keeping a special call-by-call log. Most importantly, you may want to answer the phone with, "typing service" or "word processing" to assure the potential new client that he or she is dealing with a professional operation.

It is much less expensive to have another residential line installed instead of a business line. One considerable advantage of a business line, however, is that you can be listed under "Typing" or "Word Processing" in the yellow pages and through telephone information. This is important for prospective clients who are looking up a phone number. They will probably use the yellow pages rather than the white pages for this.

You may ultimately want to expand to several phone lines. Key phone equipment is available. (You've seen it in offices—it's the phone with the little buttons that light up.) Although it is expensive, it allows you to have up to five different phone numbers on each set. This avoids the problem of having phone sets all over the house, and never knowing which one is ringing. Another option is call waiting. This feature, offered in most parts of the country, allows you to find out who is calling while you are on the line. But key sets are generally better than call waiting because they include a hold button, a signal button, and an intercom. These are especially valuable when people are working in different rooms or on different floors of a house.

You can also arrange a jump line, where, if the first number is busy, a person calling is automatically "jumped" to the next number. This helps prevent your clients from receiving busy signals.

It's a good idea to consider your future phone expansion when you start your business. When your business grows, you may be receiving dictation over the phone or transmitting word-processing files to other computers (as explained in chapter 6). Telecommunications play a central role in most business expansion so your initial consideration of phone equipment will prove important in the conversion process. You don't, for example, want to lose your phone number six months after starting your business because the services you will want are only available on other exchanges.

Today, you shop for your phone equipment as you shop for any other merchandise. The phone company no longer has a monopoly on phone equipment, so there are many private retail outlets and consultants who are willing to work with the small business proprietor.

Telephone Answering Machine

Along with your telephone, you will need a telephone answering machine to serve as your secretary when you are away. The selection of a phone answering machine is very important. It is necessary for screening calls while working and recording calls while away, and it is essential for dictation over the phone line – lucrative word-processing function.

How do you go about selecting an answering machine? Choose your machine by features first, then find the best price. Two things your machine should feature are VOX and REMOTE. Both will help you keep up with your businesses. With VOX when your machine answers, the incoming message tape keeps recording the message as long as the caller speaks, but stops a few seconds after the caller hangs up. This feature allows clients to leave long messages – even to dictate an entire letter for typing. At the same time it prevents your tape from recording annoying tone signals after hang-ups or short calls.

Since I assume you will be taking a day off now and then (an assumption not always borne out during the first year of a new business), the REMOTE feature is also desirable. This feature enables you to listen to your calls from any phone. You simply dial your own number and wait until your announcement recording plays. Then, using a portable device that comes with your machine, you rewind your tape and listen to all your messages.

Two other telephone accessories you may want to consider are the automatic dialer and the loudspeaker phone. The automatic dialer is helpful if you expect to do a lot of phone work. It enables you to dial the numbers of your clients and suppliers with a single keystroke or two. It speeds up calling and prevents a lot of wrong numbers. The loudspeaker phone lets you have a long conversation while typing or doing other work, by broadcasting the conversation over a small speaker. It is truly a device that enables you to do two things at once.

Space. In addition to considering your telephone needs, you will want to check the space you have set aside in your house or apartment. (Figure 4.1 and 4.2) This space must be adequate for client privacy and suitable for conducting your word-processing business in a professional manner. Nothing turns a client off faster than to see your unmade bed or messy bathroom while discussing the finer details of a typing job. Your work area should be separated from the rest of your apartment as much as possible. Arrangements of chairs, desk, lamps, and other furniture should create a professional office ambiance, especially with your sophisticated word processor prominently in view. The bathroom should be accessible to clients without

Courtesy of Kaypro Computer

Figure 4.1 Even a small area in the living room of your apartment can serve as a comfortable and functional word-processing office — especially with a small, portable computer, such as the Kaypro 2 pictured above.

causing you or the client any embarrassment. Partitions and bookcases are practical and inexpensive dividers. They can be used to conceal parts of your home or apartment. They can also section off your work area from your living space.

Courtesy of Valley Craft, Inc., a subsidiary of LDI Liberty Diversified Industries.

Figure 4.2 Furniture units specifically designed for today's microcomputer equipment can save considerable space in an apartment or small office.

Insurance. It is important that you carefully examine your homeowner's or tenant's insurance policy before starting your business in your home. It is possible that your present policy does not cover your equipment, since it is used primarily for business. If your apartment is burglarized, the insurance company may help replace your stereo, some jewelry, and your cameras, but they will tell you, "Sorry, your computer and telephone answering machine are business equipment. They are not covered."

Even worse, if a client trips on your oriental rug or if one of your word-processing operators falls down the stairs and breaks an arm, you may not be covered for liability. Many insurance policies exclude your business clients and personnel if the business is conducted in your home. It is imperative, therefore, that you consult with your insurance agent at the outset, honestly explaining your needs and business plans. You will probably be offered a rider to your present policy, or be shown a fairly inexpensive home-office policy. This will cover all your business equipment and offer liability protection for clients and operators while they are on your premises.

There is another insurance problem to consider as well: what if you suddenly find yourself being sued by some litigious client, who blames the spelling error in the cover letter you typed, for his failure to get a job interview? Or, what if you are sued by the frustrated doctoral student who claims the delay in handing in her dissertation is due solely to your two-day machine breakdown, rather than her three years of procrastination? These things can and do happen. I recommend, therefore, that you take a liability "umbrella" policy. This goes above all your other liability policies and offers $1,000,000 additional liability for all these strange, but real contingencies. When you are in any business, you have to expect nuisance suits, and the legal fees to defend yourself can be frightening. Even when you've done nothing to deserve it, you can find yourself in a courtroom answering the most absurd charges. Such a policy, which is fairly inexpensive will not only pay your legal fees, but give you peace of mind as well.

Working From an Outside Office

Many of the principles for working at home apply to working from an outside office but there are some differences. In an outside office, for example, you will not be able to use your residential phone service and will be required by the phone company to have a business line. You will also need a separate insurance policy. There are several other things that pertain particularly to the outside office situation.

If you are considering finding an office outside your home or apartment, several factors immediately come to mind:

Cost
Location
Availability
Competition
Conditions

Let's look at cost last (although it may be the first thing on your mind. This will help you better understand cost as one factor in a more complex picture.

Location

Your location is very important, especially if you want to attract clients off the street. One reason storefront property is so expensive is that proprietors are willing to pay for the opportunity of drawing business from passers-by in the neighborhood. Study the surrounding blocks carefully to see what businesses are around that might use your services. Are there many commercial enterprises? Is there a college or training school nearby (always an excellent source of word-processing business)? Are the people who live in the neighborhood mostly professionals who are likely to need resumes, letters, and manuscripts typed? There are a few other questions you should ask yourself with regard to the location: are you near public transportation? Is parking available? Is the location safe or will the fear of crime keep potential clients away. Each of these factors can affect your business.

Availability

Availability refers to the hours of operation. If you are planning a regular 9 to 5 routine, there is no problem. But you may want to do some of your work late at night or catch the early bird 5:53 commuter express to begin your day at the office by 7:30. Will the office space be open early and late? What about weekends? Many commercial buildings that depend on centralized heat and air conditioning do not allow you to use the facilities on weekends or holidays without a very large maintenance fee. You will have to assess the hours you will be working and the availability of the office for these hours.

Competition

Competition may also play a vital part in your decision. Are there other typing/word-processing offices nearby? Does the local copy shop offer word-processing services? Look at the local papers and community bulletin boards to see how many typists and word-processing people are advertising. Call them to find the going rate and to get a sense of what the business pulse is in that community. The fact that there are many competitors does not necessarily mean you should not consider the location. Often, a location has many competing businesses, all of which do well, because people are drawn to the area due to the selection. New York's Chinatown has over 60 restaurants with about the same menu and most of them do quite well. And, the diamond district of New York (47th Street), with over 100 diamond stores and businesses, is probably the most desired location for a new diamond shop. You must assess the effects of competition before you make your decision.

Conditions

Finally, you have to consider what I call conditions – a bunch of small factors that together weigh on your decision. What kind of lease are you being asked to sign? A one-year or two-year lease poses the danger that your rent will be doubled or tripled just as the business begins to grow. My friends opened a word-processing/copy shop an d had their rent raised from $400 per month to $1200 per month after one year. The property had not improved, but the landlord reasoned correctly, that they were making so much money they would be willing to pay the exorbitant increase. A long lease has a disadvantage, too. If you want to get out of it, perhaps to go into another business or start over in a new location, you can legally be held liable for the entire sum of the lease payments. How confident are you that your business will succeed in that location? How long can you carry the rent if the income is less than expected, as is likely in the first year of any new business.

Other "conditions" to consider are whether to go for storefront property or less expensive office space, either above a store or in an office building. You will be less visible, but you will be saving a significant sum for equivalent square footage. Also, you have to look at the potential site and realistically figure how much it will cost to fix it up in order to use it for your business.

Costs

Finally, we get to costs. How much should you spend for office space? The range I have seen is $75 per month for one person who is renting desk space in an insurance office to $3200 per month for a copy/word-processing shop on New York's fashionable upper east side. There is no easy answer, but my suggestion is to use the following formula. Decide on an amount you are willing to invest in the business without seeing a cent returned for 18 months. This is extra money you can do without. We'll call this your "throwaway" fund, and it is separate from all your other expenses. After taking into account the variables of location, availability, competition, and conditions, you can commit yourself to a lease where the sum of five months' rent is equal to your throwaway fund. This gives you a margin of safety and is pretty realistic. In other words, if after buying your word processing equipment, stationery, and taking care of your other expenses, you have $1000 left over, this becomes your throwaway fund. One thousand dollars divided by five is $200. You should not commit yourself to a rental above $200 per month.

Determining Your Business Costs

Before you can set a realistic fee schedule, you have to know what your costs are. This can be quite complicated and can involve many different factors. It can include such unpredictable things as having to retype 50 pages because of operator errors, losing text because of bad disks, clients who don't pay and sudden changes in your business expenses. The accurate determination of costs as a basis for the setting of fees is central to all business successes. I have determined some general rules that should help you come to grips with your basic cost structure.

The six main areas to consider in setting costs are: (1) overhead; (2) operator and other personnel costs; (3) computer costs, including hardware, software, and maintenance; (4) costs of consumable supplies, including ribbons, stationery, rubber bands, etc; (5) advertising; and (6) "contingencies," which are all those small and large costs that you can't predict in advance, but for which you can budget.

Different categories of costs must be assessed in different ways. I will use two examples as we go along; one that shows a person who is working from home and the other a person who has rented an outside office. These businesses are two very different kinds of operations with different goals and expectations. As a result cost structures are strikingly different.

Overhead

Overhead is a relatively fixed yearly amount that can be calculated by adding together your rent (if you are working from home this would be zero, of course), utilities related to the business, telephone and insurance. If you are not sure of these figures, you can use my figures as a general guide:

Insurance	$125 per year ($10.40 per month)
Phone	$ 25 per month
Utilities	$ 15 per month

If you are renting outside office space, these figures are tripled. Your office rent must be added to this amount along with the furnishings you've purchased for your home or outside office. If you buy furniture, figure that one-quarter of its price is its cost to you per year (or 1/48th per month). This will give you your monthly overhead costs.

Next, to compute the overhead costs per hour, you will have to know how many hours you will be working each month. If you are just starting out, or are planning a part-time business, and will work from home, estimate 50 hours per month as the time you will be doing your word-processing work. If you are using an outside office, the figure will more likely be 200 hours per month. Divide your space costs by 50 or by 200 and you have the hourly overhead for your business. From here on, the more hours you work, the higher your profit ratio, since the overhead costs don't change. Let us see how this works for Dan and Alison, two individuals who have set up their word-processing businesses, but with different focuses.

DAN: Dan, a school teacher who is trying to build a part-time business for supplemental income, is starting out small and has set up shop in his living room He partitioned off an area that has a desk and his personal computer for the word processing. His insurance agent sold him a home business policy for $110 per year, which covers his computer, office furnishings, and liability protection. He bought a couple of filing cabinets and a comfortable chair for his clients. He is hoping to do a lot of college typing business because his apartment is down the block from the campus. Here is how he computes his overhead on a monthly basis:

Office Rent	None
Insurance	9.20
Phone	35.00
Electric	10.00
Furnishings	8.20
	(1/48th of total $390 spent for furniture, including a file cabinet, chair, lamp, and coffee table on which clients can spread papers)
TOTAL:	$62.40 per month space overhead

ALISON: Alison, an enterprising young woman with an MBA and two years of corporate headaches, decided she wanted to go into business for herself. She decided to combine her good managerial, typing, and sales skills to start her own word-processing business with money she had saved during the years of her corporate work. Her goal was to develop the business over a two-year period and then sell it or get someone else to run it for her. She expected to be able to make a living from her business within six months.

First, she rented an office over a busy store in the business district of town. She had it beautifully furnished, purchasing everything on credit. Her credit included her personal department store charge cards plus a lease from a business rental company for the furniture with an option to buy after five years. She bought the best word processor available. Her philosophy, based on her corporate business experience, was that this successful image would more than pay for itself in hastening her business success. Here is how she breaks down her monthly overhead costs:

Office Rent	$350.00
Insurance	$ 40.00
Phone	$ 70.00
Utilities	$ 60.00
Furnishings	$120.00 (payments)
TOTAL:	$640.00

Operator and Personnel Costs

Whereas your overhead costs are relatively fixed, it is possible, and a good idea, to control your operator and personnel costs in relation to the business you are drawing. What this means in practice is that you are far better off using part-timers and free-lancers – independent word-processing contractors – than hiring a full-time person who may be idle when business is slow. There are two possible ways of paying your part-time or free-lance operators.

One method is to pay them by the hour. Hourly rates differ remarkably from region to region. In New York City, for example, typical free-lance word-processing operators make a minimum of $13 per hour, with higher pay on weekends, holidays, and evenings. Just 30 miles away, in Maplewood, New Jersey, the going rate for operators is $8.00 per hour. Why? Probably because the Maplewood operators don't want to travel into the city, and local proprietors realize that word-processing skills have limited marketability in the suburban area. After all, in one Wall Street building there may be 50 to 100 word processors, each representing a position. In the entire Maplewood area, there are maybe a dozen word processors, with equally few jobs. Before setting an hourly salary, you have to know what the salary range is in your area.

A second method is to pay by the job. For example, if I am charging $2.00 per page for input typing and printing a single copy, I may give the operator $1.25 and keep the rest for expenses. The speed of the operator is not as important in this kind of fee schedule since he or she is earning in direct proportion to what is produced.

I find the second method better, both for the operator and for myself. It eases tension, encourages productivity, and rewards higher performance with higher pay. Also, it can easily be computed and built into your fee schedule.

Computer Expenses

Your computer equipment will be a considerable expense in your operation, although not the largest. This expense includes your hardware, software, and maintenance contract (or service expenses if you don't have a contract). You can buy a computer or word-processing system, rent one, or lease one with an option to buy at the end of the lease. The last method is by far the best alternative for three reasons. First, it does not tie up your money. Second, you can easily compute your monthly costs. Third, it offers most people (but not all) tax advantages. There are only two reasons for not leasing. First, you should not lease if you get an exceptional deal on a direct purchase. Second, if you start your own business without a proven record you probably won't qualify for a lease. Even if the computer dealer cannot get you a lease, it is possible to get a bank loan, payable over 2 to 5 years, for your equipment and software.

If you are leasing, or if you take a bank loan to purchase, your monthly costs will be clear. Alison, for example, selected an IBM-PC computer with two double density disk drives, 256K RAM, and a fast NEC 7730 printer with a sheet feeder. Her software included the WordStar Professional Package (with MailMerge and SpellStar) and Jack 2 (for information management jobs). The whole package cost $8000.00. Due to her excellent credit rating, she got a four-year loan from her bank at 13% interest, with monthly payments of $214.62. In figuring her costs, she computes her monthly computer expenses at $250 per month, which includes what she anticipates will be her service costs (expected to be low the first year).

Dan, whose ambitions are more modest and resources more limited, bought a Kaypro 2 (bundled with the word-processing software) and the relatively slow (18cps) Silver-Reed EXP 550 printer. He paid $2400 for the package. He has decided to charge his business 1/18th the cost per month, so that it will pay for his computer system in a year and a half. This is his personal method of depreciation, again in accordance with his expectations. He figures his monthly computer costs at $160, which allows $200 per year for the service contract he purchased from the dealer.

To sum up: try to lease your equipment, and use your fixed monthly lease payment (with maintenance and software costs if they are additional) as your computer cost. If you purchase your equipment outright, I would charge 1/36th of its cost per month (which allows for interest on the money spent) as the monthly computer cost. However, if, like Dan, you expect a quicker payback, there is no reason why you cannot change this ratio.

Consumable Costs

There are costs for the supplies you will use as you do your business. While they are not large, they can add up, and should be considered a part of your business expenses.

Typical start-up costs include the following consumable expenses:

Printer ribbons (30 ribbons)	$150.00
Floppy disks (30 disks)	$100.00
Letterhead/Envelopes	$120.00
Bond paper/Draft paper	$ 80.00
Misc. stationery	$ 50.00

It is possible to break down these expenses (except your personal stationery, which might even go under advertising), on a per job basis. Or, you might want to average them out with your computer costs or general overhead. In either case, be aware that a big job may use several disks and ribbons, and these small costs do add up.

Advertising

The nature of your business and the clientele you hope to attract will determine your advertising costs. In almost all cases, I do recommend some advertising. If done correctly, it will pay for itself.

In considering your advertising needs, first look for free advertising opportunities. FREE??? Yes, there is plenty of free advertising for the taking. First, you can post public notices on local bulletin boards. Naturally, these are typed and printed on your word processor. These boards are often found in front of supermarkets, cleaners and other neighborhood stores. Colleges may have dozens of bulletin boards spread around the campus. With the appropriate permission, you can place your ads where students, eager to have their term papers typed, will take note of them. The local papers and shopping guides will sometimes give you a few weeks' free space. You must persuade them that you want to see how they draw and if they work well, you will be a regular advertiser.

By far the best type of free advertising to use is your own network of friends and professional acquaintances. When I first started my word-processing business, I was doing wills for a lawyer. He loved to sit and watch the pages of a will spew forth from the machine, chuckling at how remarkably quick it was compared to his slow-handed typist. I asked him to let his colleagues know of my work, and within a month I had a stable of clients from his building who had been referred through him.

If you are active in a church group, in the PTA or American Legion, in Hadassah or the Knights of Columbus, let your friends know about your new business and what you can do. When you go shopping on the avenue, let the storekeepers you patronize know of your new business. Tell the teachers in your child's school about it and ask them to tell their friends. You will be amazed at how word spreads and how you will build up a customer base by word-of-mouth.

Not all your advertising will be free, of course. You should decide on where to advertise according to the kind of client you want to attract. Alison was after the professional client who would come in with big jobs. Dan was eager for the local person who wanted some material typed. Alison chose to advertise in the Business Services classified section of the New York Times at a very high per line cost. Dan, on the other hand, placed a quarter page ad in the local penny shopper at about one third the price of Alison's ad. Their advertising decisions, and estimates of cost, were based on their vision of the business and the clientele they wanted to attract.

In addition to advertising in your local paper or large metropolitan dailies, some specialized advertising can be helpful. If there is a college nearby, advertising in the local paper might bring in some student or faculty business. If your word-processing business can handle specialized functions, such as legal work, advertising in law journals or law school newspapers can reach your target audience. Using your word processor to send out direct mail advertising about your business effectively demonstrates your capabilities, and shows the prospective client how the final product looks.

Contingencies

By definition, contingencies are the things you can't predict, and can therefore not quantify – but they do occur. A disk of 50 pages gets accidentally wiped out (you forgot your backup copy). A job has to be retyped because of errors. A client doesn't pay and you've already laid out the money for the operator. These things are bound to happen.

I use a simple method of adding 10% to my costs to account for contingencies. If I am computing my hourly costs, and if after adding overhead, operator salary, computer costs, and advertising, I arrive at $18.00 per hour, I add another $1.80, or 10%, as my contingency fund.

Determining Costs and Setting Fees: An Example

Earlier, we looked at how Dan and Alison set up their word-processing businesses with different goals, expectations and cost structures. Yet, despite the differences in volume and types of jobs, there will be many identical services that they will provide. The most common types include the input of several drafts of reports, contracts, documents, and dissertations; the preparation of mailing lists and letters, with the runoff of dozens of letters; and the typing and running off of resumes. Let us see how they compute their costs and set their fees for these jobs.

DAN: Dan's fees are as follows:

Input typing of double-spaced page	$1.50
Input typing of letter	6.00
Address mailing list/each item	.25
Runoff letter/per	.65
Resume (single-page)	8.00
Runoff resume/per	.65

Dan's input typing fees are less than the going rate. But, he figures, if people have to travel to use his services, they are going to expect to save some money. He has found that many clients came to him because they figured that on a 400 page dissertation, they would save between $80 and $120. Some traveled from the other side of town because they felt the savings would justify the trip.

Although Dan's input typing fees are below the going rate, his runoff fees (65 cents) are slightly above average. Might this deter some potential clients? Yes, it does, but Dan has little choice. He has computed, at the rate his printer prints, taking into account the time needed for the feeding in and the removing of papers, that he can print only 25 typical letters in an hour. Thus, he is forced to charge the higher fee. Here is how he computes his costs for the jobs:

Space overhead ($63/45 hours per month	$1.40
Operator expenses ($15 per hour for himself)	15.00
Advertising ($36/45 hours per month)	.80
Consumables (added to job)	???
Computer costs ($160/45 hours per mo.)	3.55
Contingencies	2.07
Hourly Business Expense	**$22.82**

Dan's hourly business expense reflects the nature of his business and his expectations. His overhead is remarkably small, since he works from home. However, his operator pay is at least 30% above average because he is the operator, and he expects to make $15.00 per hour for his work. This is what he would make if he worked at the after-school center and he can't see why he should make less in his own business. So, for jobs that involve his time, such as the printing jobs that depend on the slow printer, he is forced to charge higher than average fees. But because he is a fast and accurate typist, he can charge lower than average fees for the input typing. We see then that the combination of all these factors – space, operator costs, advertising, computer costs – affects what he charges and what he makes.

ALISON: Alison's fees are as follows:

Input typing of double-spaced page	$2.00
Input typing of letter	8.00
Address mailing list/each item	.25
Runoff letter/per	.50
Resume (single-page)	8.00
Run off resume/per	.50

Alison's fees reflect the structure of her business and her expectations. She runs a fully-professional operation in a high volume area. The clients she attracts are generally more interested in fast and accurate service at a convenient location rather than saving a few dollars. There are other typing and word-processing services in the area, but she knows that hers will succeed when she proves that she gets jobs done on time, even under pressure, and that they are done well.

Here is how Alison computes her hourly business expenses:

Space overhead ($640/220 hours per month)	$2.90
Operator expenses ($15 per hour for	$9.00
herself/for the operators she trained)	9.00
Advertising ($330/220 hours per month)	1.36
Consumables (added to job)	???
Computer costs ($250/220)	1.13
Contingencies	1.40
Hourly Business Expense	**15.79**

She computes her hourly costs at $15.79 and sets her basic fees at $22.00 per hour, yielding her a profit of about 30%. She calculates that if her business is operational 220 hours per month (or about 40 hours per week), she will make a clear profit of $1365 per month. Since she does most of the typing, this adds another $1800 per month, giving her a total income of $3165 per month. She can easily live on this sum.

Of course her calculations are based on the expectation that she can have her business active for 220 hours a month. If the production falls below that level, her income and profit dwindle accordingly. But even with a 50% decline, she will still make enough money to live on. And she will still be able to pay off her equipment and enjoy a sense of independence. Also, Alison has all the tax advantages associated with running one's own business.

We see, then, that a variety of factors come together in determining one's business expenses and setting costs. These factors reflect the individual nature of each person's business.

Getting Started in Business: Two Examples

To put some of these ideas in perspective and help you see how they are applied in practice, let us look at a woman who started her own successful word-processing business at home and built it into a full-time career.

Linda Marchand was pursuing a managerial career for a large New York department store when she realized that the nine-to-five regimen was not for her. Since she was a bright, energetic person with a lot of business sense, she decided to set up her own business and to work from home. She purchased a Decmate™ word processor in late 1982 and set up her business, *Words to Go* in her home in Manhattan. Two months after starting, she hired another operator with his own word processor and he worked on jobs from his home in Brooklyn.

I asked Linda what was involved in getting started and how she built the business. "The biggest thing at first," she told me, "was the courage to quit my job, buy the computer, and let the chips fall where they may." Her initial investment, including the machine, stationery, and phone, came to about $4000. "It was virtually everything I had, but I was confident enough to risk it."

When Linda started out she called everyone she knew and told them about her new business. She asked her friends in the corporate or business world to pass the word around, and in a few months her clients included some big companies. "They came to me," she explains, "because I was able to show them that it cost considerably less to use my outside service than to do many of the things they were doing in-hours." Linda was able to show them this because she had carefully computed her costs, including the profit she needed to make, and set a fee schedule accordingly. She was also familiar enough with word-processing costs to demonstrate, convincingly, that she understood the real costs of getting a job done in a company's word-processing center. "Sometimes they would compute the costs without realizing that many of the temp operators they were hiring didn't know the machine." This meant, in effect, that the real costs were double the theoretical costs. When company management realized this, they were willing to give Linda a chance to prove her cost effectiveness.

Because of the enormous cost of rental space in New York City, Linda decided to run her business from home. This is a wonderful advantage for her. As she said in a recent interview: "I can walk around in my bare feet, and I usually wear jeans and an old shirt when I'm operating – though I put on 'real' clothes when I go to see clients." But some clients take her services less seriously because she runs her business from home. She tries to make new clients feel as comfortable as possible when they come to her home. She often meets with clients at their offices, although this takes a lot more time.

How profitable can the business be? In a year she made enough to live on comfortably. Moreover, as her volume increased her profit per job increased accordingly, so the prospects for next year are even better. Linda expects to open a storefront operation soon that, in addition to providing word-processing services, will have copy machines and provide other business services.

Robert and Patricia Gibson, owners of the highly successful Park Slope Typing and Copy Service, provide another example. Patricia, the mother of a young child, had been doing typing at home to supplement Robert's income as a junior high school teacher. Robert was getting increasingly fed up with teaching and dreaded having to go to work each morning. He and Patricia decided they would start a business if they could get the money together, but they were scared. Nevertheless, the Park Slope Copy Center was opened in May, 1980. Realizing that this area, loaded with professionals, writers, and business people, did not have any place to make decent photocopies, they leased a photocopy machine and set up shop above a bagel store. They paid a very low rent since the store was not on ground level. They saved labor costs by splitting the time between them and using outside personnel as little as possible.

Soon business picked up so much that Patricia couldn't keep up with the typing, even with added staff and a new electric typewriter. She heard about my word-processing service nearby and began bringing me her big jobs: the three-hundred letters, and the long dissertations. We split the profits.

Soon it became clear to us that it was time for the Gibsons to get their own word processor and to train their own operators. I leased them a Vydec 1200 and trained Patricia on the machine. Within weeks the machine was more than paying for itself and business was booming. The word-processing service increased their copying work, and many word-processing customers bought stationery – a highly profitable item – from them. Within the year, they changed the name of their store from Park Slope Copy Center to the Park Slope Typing and Copy Center, with a large sign in the window proclaiming "Word Processing Services Offered". Within 18 months, they moved to a large storefront, on a better block, at triple the rent. Six months later, they proudly opened a second store in nearby Bay Ridge. Robert and Patricia are now in semi-retirement in the Berkshires. The business has proven so successful that they hired a full-time manager and live on the income their businesses generate for them.

I have had the opportunity to study their operation over the past four years and have seen what makes it successful. First, they contained their costs at the beginning by working long hours and hiring competent personnel as necessary. They set realistic fees, not too high but profitable enough to build the business. At the beginning, they plowed almost everything they made back into the business. They rented faster and better copiers with collators, and more sophisticated word-processing equipment to keep up with the increasing clientele. All along, they earned an enviable reputation of getting things done and getting them done right, which brought more customers to their shop. And, they kept applying their skills to expand what they did. From a simple copy shop they became a sophisticated word-processing and business-support operation, with a lucrative sideline in printed stationery and specialized note paper.

It seems to me that the elements that made Linda Marchand's and the Gibsons' businesses successful are the elements that go into all business successes. The following chapter looks further at some of the day-to-day managerial challenges in running your own word-processing business.

5

Managing Your Word-Processing Business

When you first start out, and the business basically consists of you alone, you will probably be too busy to think about management problems: problems most of us associate with large organizations or offices. As your business grows, you will find that day-to-day management can become your biggest headache. Managing your word-processing business includes training and supervising your personnel (WP operators, clerks, etc.), keeping tight control of your accounts payable and receivable, making sure you have sufficient supplies on hand, maintaining good customer relations, and all the other small details which, when added up, become the heart and soul of any business enterprise – small or large.

MANAGING YOUR OWN PROFESSIONAL LIFE

Before you even begin to think about managing the business, you have to give some serious, well-thought-our consideration to your own situation and how you interact with your business. When my friend Judy began her own word-processing business one May, for example, I asked her what she was going to do at Christmas time, because I knew she always went away for two weeks to see her family in Arizona. She laughed: "You're worried about Christmas, already. Why, I'm just getting started."

Sure enough, by Christmas time, as the business was just beginning to prosper, Judy began to realize that her business did not yet have the resources (operators, controls, and management) to run while she was away. So, she was forced to cancel her trip – an inevitability which she should have, and could have, realized right from the start.

There are several areas in which the management of your own professional life is especially important as you start a business. Assessing your personal time, your financial resources, and your intimate relationships are all critical at the beginning your venture. We will look at each of these briefly.

Managing Your Time

When you begin your business you probably have plenty of time on your hands, and can't imagine having more business than you can handle. Indeed, it is probably a fantasy of yours that the business will boom so much you will actually have to hire people. But the reality is, and I have seen it time and again, that well-run businesses do grow quickly – much more quickly than expected. In addition to planning and budgeting your money, you have to plan and budget your time.

A simple way to do this is to fill the blanks in this sentence: "I now have ____ hours per week available to devote exclusively to my business. I expect that the months of ____ and ____ will allow me more/less time. The days each week I am generally least available are _____ and _____." You can then see a general picture of the time you can presently devote to your business. In addition to this regularly allocated time, you should also leave room for contingency time, (blocks of time that you can't anticipate and that range from a couple of hours to a couple of days). If you have young children, for example, emergency baby-sitting plans should be arranged before they are actually needed. As you actually run your business you will get a better sense of the time requirements, but especially at the beginning, you should allow some flexibility for the scheduling problems and time demands that may arise.

Managing Your Financial Resources

Ideally, the monies from the business should be separate from your personal monies. The income drawn from your operation may be used to pay your expenses, invest in expanding the business or pay yourself a profit or salary check. The expenses incurred in running your business should be paid for with business earnings. That way you don't end up paying a $160.00 phone bill out of your pocket, especially when your phone bill used to be $40 before starting the business.

Unfortunately, what *should be* is not always what *is*. You may find times when, to meet your regular business expenses, especially when clients are late in paying their bills, you have to draw from your personal monies. If a large lease payment for your equipment comes due on the 15th, you can't substitute an explanation that your clients should be paying you in the next three weeks. If you need some stationery and print wheels, you can't wait until business picks up to order them. In both cases, you will have to lay out the money and pay yourself back. If you are strapped personally, have a back-up fund (maybe a parent or friend who can loan you a couple of hundred dollars at a time) so that you don't make business decisions under unrealistic pressures. Then, when you collect and tally your business monies, you can open a cushion fund to draw on in such emergencies.

You should keep careful records of what you've borrowed from friends and family, what you've loaned yourself, and what business-related bills you've paid from your personal monies – and you should see that you are paid back from the business. This will, among other things, allow you to accurately gauge how the business is doing and what profit, if any, it is showing. One colleague of mine, running her business from her apartment, claimed to be making an inordinately large profit on her business in the first three months of operation. When I inquired about how she computed this profit, I found that she regularly paid her equipment lease expenses ($260 per month) and utilities from her own money, and failed to record them among her business expenses. In the financial management discussion of this book, you will get some ideas on how to keep records – and, how to be sure that, at least for tax purposes, you are able to distinguish between your personal and business expenses.

Managing Your Personal Relationships

When you are actively engaged in building a new business, your personal life may suffer. All the energy and time channeled into this new business, all the preoccupations and daydreams about its success, all the anticipation and dread about failures and difficulties will intrude on the normal course of your personal, family, and social life.

I have seen many examples of individuals whose personal lives and business lives either collide or become too intermeshed. The best thing for you to do is maintain a perspective; a balance and ordering of priorities. Give to your business what it needs and to your personal relationships what they require. Both will then thrive.

TRAINING YOUR PERSONNEL

The next question to ask is, who can I train to run my business during those hours, days, weeks, or months that I will be least available? If the answer is no one, you will have to organize your business from the beginning to be operational on a part-time basis. For example, if your weekends are sacred to you and there is no way in the world you are going to work on Saturday or Sunday, fine. Just remember, big typing jobs, such as dissertations and legal work, often require what is handed to you on Friday to be ready Monday morning. You will have to give up jobs like these unless you can find someone to train who will be able to help you in your business.

Finding the right person, and providing the best training, is not easy, but it is not impossible. By far, the best way to recruit a potential employee for a small business is by personal referral. Ask your friends, relatives, neighbors, and others whose judgement you trust to recommend someone. Be specific about the kind of person you want, and be willing to wait until your network of friends and acquaintances finds the right person for you. It does take time. You will have to sit patiently, but the more people you tell of your needs, the less time it will take to find the right person.

What kind of person do you want? You want someone who can type, of course. It would be imprudent to attempt to train someone to type, no matter how motivated. You may not require a 70 words-per-minute typist, or one with excellent accuracy. Mistakes are easily correctable and typing speed can quickly pick up on word processor. But, the typing speed and accuracy is important in determining your method of payment to the operator.

After typing speed and accuracy, there are four things you should look for in hiring an operator. These four, in general order of importance are:

1. *Attitude.* Motivation, maturity, responsibility, and willingness to learn, as attested to by someone whose judgement you can trust.
2. *Proximity.* The closer a person lives to you, the more likely he or she will show up consistently for work, despite snow storms, transportation strikes, dead car batteries, and the other perils of commuting.
3. *Language skills.* Oral and written communication skills are an advantage in this type of business. You want a person who can proofread, avoid spelling errors, demonstrate good judgement, and speak well on the phone and in person with your clients.
4. *Previous training or experience on a word processor.* It does not matter if the person operated the same system as you are presently using, or another system. Anyone who has proficiently operated one system can usually learn another system relatively quickly. If you are going to be providing training, the proof of a person's aptitude to learn is their previous experience on some word-processing system.

Are you likely to find a person who can meet all these requirements? Yes, although there may be some trade-offs. You can decide, from your own business needs and personal perspective, which skills are most important to you and which can be improved through on-the-job training.

There are two caveats to consider as you look for someone. The response from friends and acquaintances may be, "I've been looking for part-time work. Why don't you hire me." While it is not always a bad idea to hire your friends, it is risky enough to make you think twice before doing it. I have often hired friends and family for my own operation. Statistically, it has worked out successfully at about the same percentage rate as hiring outsiders. But – and this is a big but – when it doesn't work out with your friends, you don't just lose an employee; you sever or strain what was an amicable relationship. There is no severance pay for emotional ties.

The second caveat involves employment agencies. I have found, on the whole, that they are honest and reputable, but I've gotten burned enough times to be cautious. They did, on one occasion, send a person for on-the-job, paid training (2 weeks) who they knew would be moving away in a month. On another occasion, they sent a young man, who they represented as a qualified and experienced Vydec word-processing operator. It turned out that he had just completed an introductory 12 hour course and had no experience. The employment agency is often more interested in its placement commission than in your professional needs. They should generally be avoided or dealt with cautiously.

One alternative to using your personal network is to advertise in the papers. Local newspapers, which will be read by people who live close to you (remember, proximity is number 2 on our list), are less expensive and more reliable than the large city dailies, but they don't reach the same broad readership. You may, after trying the local paper, have to advertise in the classifieds of the metropolitan papers. In either case, specify in the ad whether you want part-time or full-time, where you are located (if not downtown), and general qualifications. A typical classified ad may look like the example on the following page.

WORD PROCESSING OPERATOR

Small local business needs word-processing operator to work approx. 20 hours per week. Hours flexible, salary negotiable. Call (201) 555-1212 in Maplewood for appointment.

This ad gives enough information, without being too specific, to attract reasonably qualified individuals looking for work.

Some Training Guidelines

If you are lucky enough to find an operator with experience on your particular system, you can skip this section. But with so many different software programs and machines available, the odds are in favor of having to train your operator.

The first question to ask is whether you will pay the operator during the training period, or begin paying after training. My general policy (after some previous bad experiences) is to not pay an operator during the training period. I explain at the outset of the interview that I will be providing free training to the person. As a result, he or she will have a very marketable job skill, even if the decision is not to work for me. I also tell the person that not everyone who begins the training can complete it, but that if he or she has had experience on another machine, there is more than a 90% chance of success. The training takes between 20 and 40 hours and I usually spread it over two weeks. While some applicants need a job and money right away, most of them understand that, in lieu of salary, they are gaining a very valuable skill for their investment in time.

The second question is when to squeeze in training time. If you are truly in need of an operator, then it is likely that your word processor is chugging along full steam, you are harried by your clients' unreasonable demands, and you have neither the patience nor the available machine-time to provide training. If you have more than one machine, of course, the problem is solved since you can train an operator on one while doing your own work on another – but most of us are not that fortunate.

I have generally found that the best way to train is to organize your training around real jobs, but not overly complex ones. Then you can be present to supervise while the trainee actually does the work. In this way, the work gets done – albeit at half the speed – while the person learns the system. For instance, I had to train a new operator in a week during which my machine was overloaded with work. The work involved typing a doctoral dissertation, sending out a mass mailing of business letters, preparing several resumes, compiling a statistical corporate report and creating and filling in a database system for a dairy. I decided to divide each of these jobs into small, manageable chunks and train my new operator on all these different functions. I decided that four hours a day was a reasonable time for the training.

On Monday, my regular operator typed fifteen pages of the dissertation, and I spent four hours teaching my trainee how to input and store the information. He also saw footnoting, and super- and subscripts. About six pages got typed in the four hours, but the six pages were an extra benefit of the training. On Tuesday, my regular operator began typing in the mailing list for the mass mailing. When she left, I spent one-and-a-half hours with my trainee, typing the dissertation to reinforce what we did the day before. I then moved him on to mailing-list typing and he finished up what was left of the mailing list. On Wednesday morning, my regular operator was able to begin the runoff of the list and letter, since the trainee had completed the input typing. When he came by in the evening, I had him run off some more letters and do all the envelopes. In the hour remaining, I had him review the input dissertation typing, since that job would go on all week. By now, he was fully competent on text inputting and formatting and was beginning to get a sense of the machine's logic and idiosyncrasies (he did, I must mention, have a year's experience as a word-processing operator on another machine and he was a good learner). Thursday, I began to teach him the software for database and Mail-Merge, and he spent an hour typing two resumes. On Friday, he worked six hours and went over everything with me. After the weekend, he was ready to begin work as a paid operator, even though he would still need some additional on-the-job training.

This system works because you, as the owner, see your jobs getting done and your backlog dwindling, while at the same time your new operator is being trained. You don't feel the frustration and anxiety you would experience if your jobs lay dormant while your operator was being trained. But be sure you closely supervise every step, since even the best trainee is likely to make mistakes that could seriously damage a big job.

ACCOUNTS AND EXPENSES

If you have been receiving a salary, you are in for a few surprises when you begin running your own business. Money is always coming and going – missing or in the mail – potential or realized. Money becomes, in any business, a central variable of how well or poorly the business is doing, and where it is going. While there are many aspects of money over which you will have little control, in this section we will examine those aspects that you can, and should, control as you run your business.

The first rule is *keep careful records of everything*! From the very beginning of your business, you should record every single expense, no matter how small, with a notation of how the money was spent. I call this an expense log, and it can easily be set up on your computer. The following table shows an expense log for someone starting out. Some of your expenses will be large chunks (the purchase of your equipment or office furniture) and in your reference column you should make note of how much, per month, you are charging to the business. Some expenses may be divided between personal and business uses. For instance, if you are using your regular phone (which I do not advise), you have to figure out what percentage of your bill is chargeable to business and what percentage is chargeable to personal use.

Expense Log -- First 30 Days of Business

Date	Check#	Amount	Pay To	Reference
3/1	288	55.80	New Jersey Bell	Installation and first month service
3/5	291	116.44	Pk. Slope Copy	Stationery
3/19	300	44.00	Pi Communic.	Ad. in Villager
3/23	303	180.00	H. Miller	Typing job (Black's dissertation)
3/27	309	14.56	Krell Stat.	Misc. office supplies

These expense records are important for three reasons. First, they will enable you to plan budgets in the future based on a realistic expense profile. Second, they show you how profitable your business is, or how much you will have to gross in order to reach the break-even point. And, the final, and most compelling reason, is that all businesses have a silent partner from the beginning. This partner, the IRS, is out to get whatever percentage of your monies it can. You will be realizing enormous tax advantages as you run your business. To back them up you will have to maintain accurate and honest records of everything you spend, how it relates to the business, and what you receive. Starting this practice from the beginning will save you many woes later on.

When you have your own business, you also have to be alert to the municipal, state, and county regulations regarding business practices, licenses, and permits. It is a good idea to consult a business lawyer or accountant to find out if you are required to pay a fee to the town, or display any kind of license on your property. If you are earning a regular income, from which no tax is withheld, you will have to pay estimated quarterly payments to the State and Federal tax authorities.

Keeping Track of Income

Records of your income should be just as detailed and accurate as the records of your expenses. The following table shows how I recommend you keep these records.

RECORDING OF BUSINESS INCOME

Date	Client	Amount	Job	References
3/5	Robt. Stone	56.90	Ltr/Rsm	Check #2100 Citibank Disk 5
3/8	Valley Insurance	189.00	Letter	Bill Sent 3/8 Disk 3
3/11	Daisy Wheeler	8.00	Resume	Cash (disk 3)
3/13	Carter Auto Body	11.00	Typing	Check 4567 (MHT) Disk 5
3/17	Dan Johnson	27.50	Res/Ltr	Bill sent 3/17 Disk 4

In addition to the name of the client and brief description of the type of job, the table indicates the method of payment (a check from Citibank) and where the material is stored (disk 5). If the client comes back six months later to have the work updated, you will be able to find it immediately, know what you charged last time, and know if that client's credit is good. You might also indicate on the chart if you have stored a mailing list or information from a database that could prove useful on another job. For example, whenever I do a job that involves a college or legal firm mailing list, I make note of this, since these types of lists are typically used time and again.

Using a Database/Accounting Manager

You can keep these kinds of tables electronically through your computer or word processor. All you need is the appropriate software (see Figure 5.1). You will find that you have accurate records, and you will be able to retrieve information in any form. You will be able, at the end of the year, to generate a list of all your expenses, broken down according to different deductible categories. You will also, at any time, be able to see how much a client spent in a year and provide a receipt for the client if requested. This can all be done easily with the right software.

For example, there is an excellent software package called HOME ACCOUNTANT (Continental Software), which runs on Apple or Franklin, IBM, and compatible machines, Zenith/Heath and some CP/M systems. This single package records all incoming and outgoing expenses and reconciles your checking records with your bank balance. It allows you to search for specific transactions and to sort your information by category or criterion (such as all the resume jobs done in May). It also provides graphs to show you how your business is doing, how your income and expenses balance out, or how a specific phase of your busi-

Courtesy of Epson of America, Inc.

Figure 5.1 You can keep your business records, and analyze your monthly performance and profit on your word processor. Software such as Lotus 1-2-3 and Context MBA will help you with these functions.

ness is doing. HOME ACCOUNTANT is a relatively easy program to learn, and rather inexpensive considering what it offers.

Credit and Collections

You will find that many clients, especially those that are business-oriented, are used to dealing with at least 30 days credit. They will be interested in working out an ongoing credit arrangement with you, whereby you do the job now and they pay you within 30 days. Establishing a credit policy from the outset is important in the total management of your income and the maintenance of good client relations.

First you must decide if you should extend credit or not. There is no question that the extension of credit is a positive factor in your business. Many people will use more of your services if they don't have to pay up front. There is also no question that you have to write off some losses if you extend credit, since not everyone will pay and only a percentage will pay promptly. If you have to put up the money to pay your operators, you will have to be very patient until you can even recoup your expenses. Also, it is more difficult to manage your cash flow if accounts are outstanding, and you are not sure when the money will be coming in.

If you decide not to extend credit, however, you will lose some of the business clients who are used to dealing with credit arrangements. Of course, you could be selective and extend credit to businesses and professionals, but not to the student who is having a dissertation typed. Unfortunately, my experience shows that the business client, even the large business, is often as tardy in making payments as the college student. In short, there is no way to be sure.

One possible compromise is to accept charge cards. The larger cards, VISA and Mastercard, will not extend credit privileges if you work out of your home or if you do not have a proven credit rating and business experience. You should check the requirements, since charge cards are a perfect compromise between the extension or refusal of credit.

Once you do extend credit, you will have to work out a model for collections. Even the most responsible clients will not send their check at the end of the month if they don't get a bill. Fortunately, when you have a microcomputer or word processor, the task of keeping track of all monies due is made easier with what is called *accounts receivable* software. The Peachpack 4™, which sells for less than $400, is an excellent package that will not only maintain your accounts receivable and accounts payable records, but is powerful enough for you to offer some bookkeeping services to your word-processing clients.

In addition to your record keeping, you will want to have some letters to send to clients whose payments are over due. Ideally these letters must represent a delicate blend of encouragement for them to pay without offending them enough to lose their business. There are several excellent books on the market (including Arnold S. Goldstein's *Getting Paid* that offer the small business proprietor detailed information on how to collect the money that is due.

CUSTOMER RELATIONS

Almost everyone I talk to in the word-processing business has a story – or several stories – to tell about the unreasonableness of some of their clients. There is the woman who came in to have 300 resumes and cover letters individually typed for her son. He had just graduated from law school and was applying for a legal job. After this massive job was run off, she decided she didn't like the type style and asked to have it completely redone, eagerly willing to pay twice, "plus a bonus for your inconvenience." By the time it was run off the second time, now 1200 sheets in all, the son had found a job and the woman was unwilling to pick up the work, or pay for it. The word-processing proprietor was left with 1200 worthless sheets of resumes and letters and a night in small claims court.

What do clients complain about? The main things are:

1. The job is not done quickly enough.
2. The work is too expensive. They could get it cheaper elsewhere (so why don't they?)

3. It doesn't look like they expected it to.
4. They want to make changes but not pay for having the job run off again.
5. They find a typo and, even though you are willing to run it off for free, they rant and rave about how such a thing could have happened.
6. Anything and everything else!

While there is no way to avoid customer complaints, or at least I have not discovered the way, there are some good business practices that can lead to more satisfied customers (see Figure 5.2) and fewer conflicts.

Courtesy of Digital Equipment Corporation

Figure 5.2 Effective customer relations include understanding the psychological as well as the word-processing needs of the client. Making the client feel a part of the process is a good beginning for an effective business relationship.

First, I have found that using a written clarification sheet, something between a written contract and oral agreement, lessens confusion later on. While this is not a signed contract, it is presented to the client to read and agree with. The form I've developed takes into account the major areas of controversy and is written in simple English.

In addition to this written clarification, good customer relations are primarily maintained by good communication between the proprietor and the client. People will often come to you in an excited state. You have to be part psychologist to calm them down and get them to clearly understand what you can and cannot do for them, a realistic due date for the job, and the possible things that can go wrong. In short, you have to anticipate trouble before it happens.

EMPLOYEE RELATIONS

While you are maintaining positive relations with your clients, you must also foster an honest and productive relationship with each of your employees. Far more than typing speed and word-processing competence, the right attitude is the single most critical factor in how well or how poorly an employee will perform.

There are three principles I have found helpful in maintaining good employee relations. First, I intentionally set myself up as a role model for my employees. I never ask them to do anything I would not do myself, no matter how unpleasant. For example, one time an operator ran off 40 letters on a bond that was slightly off the color that the customer wanted. I noticed it as the job was being packed, and pointed it out to the operator. I could see immediately that she was upset, and considered the problem too trivial to require rerunning the job on her own time. "Do you think the customer will notice?" she asked, hinting that maybe we could get away with it. But since I want my employees to

---

WORK AGREEMENT

1. The work submitted consists of ____ which will be approximately ____ single/double spaced typed pages.
2. The work will be typed exactly as submitted. Any typographical errors, spelling or grammatical mistakes, or other errors in the original will be the client's responsibility when they are transferred to the final copy. Costs of retyping will be the client's responsibility. However, the word-processing operator will make efforts to correct what he/she sees as obvious errors in spelling or grammar, unless otherwise instructed by the client.
3. The work should be completed by ____, barring equipment breakdown or unpredictable problems. Some jobs take longer than expected and, although we will try our best to have it ready on the above date, no promise is made that it will be ready then.
4. The estimated cost of the job is ____. This represents our rate of ____ per page for typing and ____ per page for printing. The client will pay the entire fee on receipt of the completed job.
5. The client agrees that once the job or any part of it has been done, the client is responsible for paying for the job or the part of it that has been done, even if the client no longer needs the material or informs us of a cancellation before the job is completed. However, if the client cancels before the job has been started, the client will not have to pay at all.

---

strive for perfection, not to just "get by", I wanted the job rerun. Rather than risk her ire and the development of a negative attitude, I offered, insisted, in fact, to do the runoff myself. "I'm a little crazy about these kinds of things," I explained, almost apologetically. "I guess I'm what you'd call a compulsive personality." We joked about it as I began running the job off a second time. The joking discharged the anxiety she felt at watching her boss redo the job she had botched. But the point was clearly made – and it was made in a way that was nonpunitive and nonthreatening to her. She saw that I was willing to do unpleasant work in order to achieve a final product that was consistent with the quality of my business. So, simultaneously she learned my philosophy and felt that she would not be exploited to attain it.

A second principle is to be sensitive to your employee's needs, feelings, expectations, mood swings, and idiosyncratic moments. When we work 10 hours a day with word processors and computers, we get used to predictable certainty. When the machine breaks down, we curse, complain, and call the service technician. When the machine is printing, we expect a smooth 50 pages an hour to pop out of the printer. In other words, we set ourselves into a production routine from which it is uncomfortable to deviate.

Operators and employees are not machines. They have good days and bad days. They handle some jobs better than others. They make foolish mistakes for which there is no excuse. They get tired in the afternoon and perky by dusk when it's time to go home. In short, they are human.

I try to keep a sensitive eye on my operators. If thing are getting botched, I don't explode and accuse. Instead, I take a half hour from a job and have a heart-to-heart talk to find out what is troubling the employee, and what can be done about it. The worst things to do when an employee is upset is to bend to the time pressure. You will want to; it is difficult to resist stepping up pressure when the work goes slowly. But I have found, from the point of view of productivity and human relations, that taking time out to talk to your employee can resolve problems that are slowing down the work. These talks also lessen potential resentment and discontent. Whether it is boyfriend/girlfriend trouble, feelings about the job, work conditions, or anything else, and honest heart-to-heart talk can be the most powerful palliative there is.

Finally, my third principle of effective employee relations is to treat the employee fairly, in terms of salary, hours, and conditions. When I had two machines, one in a warm spot of the house and one in a cold room, I sat at the cold machine so my operator could work comfortably. When I agreed to a fixed price for a job, but the job turned out to be twice the trouble we had anticipated, I paid the operator twice as much and lost my profit. In the short run, you can get away with mistreating your employees. In the long run, it will have a detrimental effect on your business.

SUMMING UP

This chapter examined the attitudes, behaviors, policies, and practices that contribute to the effective management of your business. The assessment and management of your own time and resources is central in realistically understanding the scope and potential of your business. You have to appropriate time and funds to keep the business running smoothly, during slow times and fast, through the vicissitudes of fortune and famine that affect any business.

The selection and training of your operators will ultimately determine to what extent the capabilities of your hardware and software are used. Almost any equipment you purchase is more powerful than the use made of it.

The management of a business involves a detailed sense of money management. Careful accounting of all your income and expenses is possible by using the right software that will keep these records for you. This information can be categorized by criteria that are important for preparing your tax returns, in evaluating your business flow, and for breaking down your profit ratio realistically. You should also decide on a credit policy, and if you do extend credit, collections of accounts receivable will be an issue with which you will have to come to terms.

6

Beyond Word Processing

The first thing most people think about when they consider word processing as a business is the input typing of client-produced material (term papers, business reports, letters, dissertations, resumes, etc.) and the printing out of the material on a typewriter-quality printer. This is probably the single largest application and one that offers you many business opportunities. But it is not the only one, as we are going to find out in this chapter.

I mentioned earlier that running your own word-processing business can involve much more than simply inputting, editing, and running off material. In fact, many individuals make the bulk of their income from the ancillary services they provide as part of a comprehensive word-processing business.

This chapter goes beyond the basic typing services and looks at the range of opportunities for a word-processing business. It will help you to assess which opportunities are most suitable and profitable for you. Throughout, try to ask yourself how *your* skills, interests, personal/social and professional networks, and your training and competencies mesh with the opportunities available. By the end of this chapter, you will have explored five different areas for a word processing business:

1. preparing clients' letters and compiling targetted mailing lists
2. resume preparation and resume typing
3. word processing and database management support for businesses and educational institutions
4. research and bibliographic assistance
5. word-processing training

LETTERS AND MAILING LISTS

Many of the clients who come to you will be people who are applying for jobs, starting their own businesses, raising money for organizations, or engaged in a professional endeavor which involves sending out large numbers of individually typed letters. Since typing these letters could take weeks and carries the likely risk of many mistakes, they come to a word-processing center where the letter will be automatically typed, over and over, with consistent accuracy and superhuman speed.

Generally, these clients are interested in two things: they want the letter to look good and they want it ready quickly. They will examine all your type face styles and fine bond papers (if they are not using their own letterheads), and ask you to make samples of what their letter will look like. They will love the justification feature, where the right column is aligned evenly. Using this feature on a letter tells the reader immediately that it was done on a word processor so it is usually not recommended for mass mailing jobs. Next, the client will want the letter ready for mailing quickly, probably by yesterday. Once the urge strikes a client to write the letter and the time has been spent doing it, delays caused by you are not appreciated. "Always be prepared for unreasonableness," should be your motto.

There are three basic parts to the letter/mailing list job:

1. Typing the letter into the computer.
2. Typing in the mailing list.
3. Printing the letters (by merging the letter and names and addresses from the mailing list.

You will see shortly how you can earn about twice the amount of money by adding two other functions to those listed above. But first, let's look at how those three work and how you should set your pricing schedule.

The typing (inputting) of the letter is a simple, direct job that is basically the same as typing a page of any document. There will be codes within the letter for the inserts from the mailing list. Inserts always include the inside address and part of the salutation. Sometimes, material is inserted in the body of the letter, such as the company name, to personalize each letter. If the material included within the body is lengthy (over, say 25 characters), then that paragraph in each letter may have to be readjusted each time. For instance, if I am inserting the name of a company in a key place in the letter, two different company names will produce lines like these:

1. . . .sending my material to Brown's fabrics in the hope that. . .
2. . . .sending my material to William J. Patterson and Sons, Inc. in the hope that. . .

In the second example, the longer company name produces a longer line which requires the paragraph to be readjusted or reformed after the insert.

All these things should be explained to your clients. It will help them understand what you are doing and why you are charging what you are. I typically charge $8.00 for the inputting of a letter. You may say, "Isn't that a bit steep when you only charge $2.25 for the inputting of a regular typed page?" Perhaps so, but people rarely complain about that particular cost. They realize that for one small fee they are in effect having the letter typed and stored on the computer disk and it will be available for them as often as they need it. I also justify the fee by explaining that the operator has to know special codes in order to do the letter properly. Due to the increased complexity of this task, it is prone to error and retyping.

The typing in of the mailing list and inserted material is a different story. Here, you need a special mailing list or MailMerge software and your operator has to know how to use it. Before typing begins, it is imperative that the client and you fully understand just what is going to be inserted and where. The complexity of your MailMerge software will help determine your price, but I generally charge 25 cents per inside address and salutation, with additional charges for other inserted material. My operators can typically type in 50 or more entries per hour, which means that this charge just about pays their salaries and covers the overhead expenses (see chapter 4). Keeping this fee reasonable, I find, is psychologically important in encouraging the client to add more names to the mailing list without fear of incurring inordinate expenses.

I make most of my profit on the printing of the letter. I figure that my printer, with a sheet feeder, can print 50 letters per hour. A full-fledged operator is not needed during the printing phase. I use a young assistant who is paid $5.00 per hour to watch the machine, press a few buttons and add paper and envelopes. I charge 60 cents per letter for printing which results in a gross of about $30 per hour. From the client's perspective, aside from the one-time inputting fee, each letter costs 85 cents (25 cents for inside material and 60 cents for the printing).

After salary and other expenses (machine time and use, lighting, electric, etc.), I estimate my profit at $20 per hour. If I can keep my machine going on a print schedule for four hours a day I earn enough to keep myself and my employees in business. If you are a large enough operation, one machine will do just this eight hours a day or more, adding another $80 profit to the coffers each day. Printing is typically the most profitable part of the business.

Let us consider a typical example. A client, who is applying for a job, comes in with a one-page letter and a mailing list of 50 people to whom she wants to have the letter sent. The costs for the client are:

Inputting of the letter	$ 8.00
Typing of the list (50 at .25)	12.50
Running off (50 at .60)	30.00
TOTAL	$50.00

The total real cost to the client is $1.01 per letter, a much lower cost than individually typed letters and, of course, a more accurate job. The more letters she has printed, the lower the cost per letter.

Let's look now at my profits. It takes the operator, who makes $12.00 per hour, ten minutes to type in the letter. That costs me $2.00 plus $1.00 for expenses and contingencies. That leaves $5.00 profit. Let us assume that I make no profit on the input of the mailing list. The runoff job is another $20 profit (cost minus labor and expenses). Thus, my profit on this $50.50 job is $25.00, or about half. Since the client is getting such a good deal, compared to typing, she will certainly recommend my services to others.

A Better Idea

If these basic services look good, there is a way to make almost twice as much profit on the same job and provide additional services to your clients. Whether you can do this or not depends on your skills and your available time.

Here is how it works. In addition to inputting the letter and mailing list and printing the finished letter, you can offer two more profitable items:

- researching and preparing a mailing list.
- helping prepare the cover letter.

These are natural extensions for this type of job. You will find that most of your clients put together a mailing list rather haphazardly, using telephone books, advertisements from newspapers, assorted clippings and notes. They don't know how to find an accurate, up-to-date mailing list in a professional way. But if you know how, you can offer them the service of preparing a thorough mailing list in addition to inputting the mailing list and merging it with the letter. This is a highly skilled service and, for the amount of time it requires, quite profitable. I find about 20% of my clients use this service and are willing to pay the premium price for it.

Mailing lists can be compiled through the use of specialized directories available in most libraries. Although there are literally hundreds of directories, the following main ones are usually all you need. They will help you compile mailing lists in six different professional areas, where word processing jobs are most likely to be found.

Legal. You can obtain a listing of all the major law firms, including names of partners and associates from the *Martindale-Hubbard Directory.* Divided into geographical categories, this reference work describes the type of law practice, the size of the firm, and other relevant information. It allows for the preparation of a legal firm mailing list tailored to your client's needs.

Business, Corporate. Thorough listings of large businesses and corporations, along with their managers and directors, can be found in *Standard & Poors Directory of American Businesses.* Dun & Bradstreet also has a directory that lists businesses according to their major emphasis. Either of these, along with the area yellow pages, will allow you to prepare a mailing list for the client looking for a position in the corporate world.

Sales and Promotion. There are over 500 major directories and reference works that can accurately target a mailing list for the salesperson trying to reach a specialized market or the client involved in product or service promotional activities. For example, one colleague of mine prepared a mailing list of over 1,000 knitting mills in the United States and Canada for his dye salesman. The list was gathered from *Davison's Knit Good Trades (The Red Book)*, which is a comprehensive directory of mill listings. Computer and information specialists can get lists from *Data Communications Buyer's Guide* or *Datapro Reports.* These, and thousands of others, are listed in the *Directory of Directories,* a comprehensive reference work that lists tens of thousands of invaluable directories in business, industry, labor, education, science, technology, engineering, recreation, government, and the social sciences. This single work lists virtually every major directory published in the United States and Canada, with a detailed description of what the directory includes. I find this one of the single most valuable reference books on my shelf.

Colleges, Graduate and Professional Education, Teaching. There are a number of excellent guides available which list all the major colleges, universities and professional training schools in the United States. Both the *(Barron's)* and *(Lovejoy's)* guides have reputations for being up-to-date and comprehensive. I suggest that you record your mailing list through a database management system which can be merged with your word processor. This way, for future jobs, you will be able to select specific schools that meet the client's defined criteria; such as schools in the Northeast region or schools that emphasize engineering. I have found this mailing list to be the one most commonly requested by clients.

Fund Raising. The *(Foundation Directory)* and *(Foundation Grants Index)* provides opportunities to learn of the major philanthropic organizations with endowments and grants. However, local fund raising efforts (a local church or community organization) are better handled with a mailing list of individuals in the community. Such a mailing list can usually be purchased inexpensively from a local newspaper that maintains a file of such lists.

Publishing, Writing, Editing. There are three important directories in this area that will help you assemble an up-to-date mailing list for an editor, proofreader, writer, sales executive or advertising person. The most important is *(LMP), Literary Market Place.* This yearly reference work includes both large and small publishers, their addresses and their main editorial, production and business personnel. In addition, it describes the types of books published, the number of titles released each year and other pertinent information. *LMP* also provides lists of free lance editors, agents, and printing and photocomposition places, covering every aspect of professional book publishing. It is a valuable guide to all areas of publishing.

For mailing lists directed more specifically to the periodical publishing trade, *Magazine Industry Market Place (MIMP)* is ideal. This comprehensive guide is the key reference tool to the editorial and publishing personnel in the United States and Canada. It lists every major publication and categorizes each by the type of material emphasized. It provides the names of editors and gives some information about the periodical. It is designed primarily for people working in the magazine publishing industry, and provides the names of officers and supervisory personnel at virtually all magazines. If your client has background in the art department of a magazine, you can prepare from *Magazine Industry Market Place* a list of all the art editors in the country or a list that is specific to a geographical region.

The *Directory of Associations* is useful in the publishing related areas as well as other areas. It lists over 35,000 professional, trade, cultural, educational, governmental, religious, recreational and other types of associations in the United States. Over half of these organizations have a publishing arm or function, publishing either newsletters, periodicals or professional journals, books, or public relations literature. If a client is looking for a position in the publishing area, the *Directory of Associations* can offer a comprehensive listing.

In addition to helping the client prepare the mailing list, you can make additional money by helping the client write an effective business letter. This is a highly profitable service and one welcomed by clients lacking in writing skills. In a following section, we will look more closely at how good writing skills can be a valuable asset in a word processing business; in the preparation of cover letters, business letters, and resumes.

Setting Your Mailing List Fee

How do you set a fee for this work? Should you charge by the hour or by the entry? Before deciding on your fee, it is important to determine how useful the list will be to you in the future. Let's say you spend six hour researching, collating, and typing a compiled mailing list from *Standard &, Poors Directory*. The next time you have a client with similar needs, assuming it is not years later, you already have your mailing list typed in and incur no extra expenses in providing it to the client. It is important then to assess how useful this mailing list is to your business: is it likely to be used again or is it too specific for most other jobs and, therefore, a one-time application?

With this in mind, you work out your fee. I always try to avoid hourly charges since they often result in the client's suspicion that the person is working slowly and increasing the cost of the job. "It should have been done in less time," they say, without knowing what is involved. I have found that a charge of 50 cents per entry (25 cents for typing in and 25 cents for researching) is adequate and generally acceptable to most clients. This adds to their per letter cost (now $1.26), but is still cheaper than having it typed. They are also assured of having a mailing list that is current. The profit is about 12 cents per entry (50%) assuming that you know which directory to go to and how to make your selections. When the second client comes and needs the same list, the profit jumps to 25 cents per entry (100%) for researching, and jumps to 25 cents for the input typing (another 100%) since the work only has to be done once. The mailing lists I find I use over and over again are, in order: Colleges and Universities, Publishers (including book and periodicals), Corporate Personnel and Sales. My college mailing list was typed once, is updated every 18 months or so, and resold about ten or fifteen times a year. Clients who purchase this list include individuals applying for college or graduate school admission, looking for professional or administrative positions, or selling something (from text books to sweat suits) to colleges or universities. Remember, you can always modify a large mailing list file by deleting some items or selecting items by criteria (corporations specializing in textiles, for instance), assuming your software is capable of performing the task.

SUMMING UP: MAILING LISTS

We have covered a lot in this section and it is worth the effort since the mailing list and letter function is likely to make up at least half of your total business. It is also generally the least risky part, since you are not dealing with dozens of individually typed pages, rife with potential errors. The following list summarizes the five key services, plus pricing and profits, in this area.

1. **Typing in of letter.** This is a one-time only job, but about three times as profitable as regular document typing. I charge $8.00 for the input of a single-page letter. Profit is approximately 62%.

2. **Typing in of mailing list.** This is not a highly profitable part of the process and I write it off as a "break even." But it generates the income from the printing, so the more you type in, the more you will print. I charge 25 cents per entry, which includes the inside address. Other inserts require an additional charge.

3. **Printing of letters.** This is profitable, especially if you don't rely on your high-priced operator to do the job. A lesser qualified and lower paid person can handle the printing. I charge 60 cents a letter for printing, approximately 65% of which is profit.

4. **Preparation of letter.** This requires a special skill. You have to know how to write a good letter. If you do, it can be profitable. I charge by the hour for this service since I am sitting down and working with the client directly. It usually runs about $50 for 1 1/2 hours of work and thought.

5. **Compiling the mailing list.** Again, you need the skill and knowledge to go to the right place and find your material quickly but, there is no reason why

you can't learn to do this. I charge 25 cents per item for the compiling, about 50% of which is profit the first time. For additional uses of the mailing list, the profit margin approaches 100%.

RESUME PREPARATION

Next to letters and mailing lists, resumes will probably be your largest source of word-processing business. Savvy job applicants in today's competitive job market realize that a professionaly typed resume has an edge over photocopies. While some clients will want to have their resumes printed rather than produced by word processing, they should be discouraged from this for two reasons. First, once a resume is printed, to make even small changes (such as adding another line of job description or an additional reference) requires the whole resume be reprinted. This is both expensive and time consuming. Second, word processing offers a major advantage in flexibility: a client can have two or three versions of a resume, typed into the machine each one emphasizing different aspects of his or her background and abilities, and geared to a specific job area. For instance, one of my clients, a teacher, had four different versions of her resume prepared, each offering the same information but with different emphasis. One resume highlighted her career as a special education teacher; one her administrative abilities in the educational setting; one her part-time experience over the past five years in real-estate sales; and the last highlighted her background using computers in the classroom. For each of the different types of jobs to which she applied, she had a resume that highlighted her specific abilities in that area.

The resume business can be highly profitable because it essentially involves one single input typing job. The remaining work consists of running off the resume which, as mentioned before, is the most profitable part of the word processing business. I charge $8.00 for inputting a one-page resume, twice that for a two-page job, and 60 cents a page for running it off. Invariably, with most resume jobs, come cover letter jobs which generate the same high profits as the resumes.

Even more profit can be made if you help your clients prepare their resumes. Just as most clients need help in assembling a mailing list or writing a cover letter, they also need assistance preparing their resume. If you have a skill that can help them, they are generally willing to pay a nice fee for it. I charge between $50 and $100 for resume preparation; an added bonus above my word-processing fees.

Many of your clients, objective and dispassionate in their professional endeavors, will experience a tremendous amount of difficulty and procrastination in getting their cover letters and resumes in shape. There is a tendency to overidentify with one's own resume; to view it too much as a reflection of who one is and what one has done. Clients benefit by seeking the advice of a truly objective person who can approach the task of resume preparation with an unbiased eye; someone who recognizes that a good cover letter or resume is not necessarily the longest or most detailed.

You don't need a lot of training to help people prepare good resumes. Common sense, some psychological understanding, a willingness to listen to the client, and a few practical principles should be able to get you started in the resume-preparation business. Your clients' successes in getting interviews based on the resume you prepared will build up your business from that point. Your understanding of what a resume is, and what it does, is central to your ability to approach the task correctly.

Myths and Facts About Resumes

Although a good cover letter and resume can be an important help in getting a job interview, they are not in themselves the way to a job and should never be viewed as such. Yet, the task is often approached with such trepidation, you would think a life is on the line. Individuals put off for weeks getting started on their resumes and experience headaches, stomach cramps, and nightmares when they think about it. When they finally do get started, they can't stop themselves from writing a ten-page autobiography instead of a one-page summary. Their cover letters suffer from the pains of introspection, the conceits of bombast, and the vague prescience that if they stop writing and finally end, the reader will crumple the letter and throw it in the waste basket.

If you, as the professional, view preparing a resume or cover letter as a means to an end, with an objective detachment beyond the client's biased perspective, you will be of enormous help to your client.

Here are a few resume myths and facts that should help you put the resume in perspective.

MYTH	FACT
A resume should show the prospective employer that this is the perfect person for the job.	The main purpose of a resume is not to sell yourself or make yourself seem perfect for the job, but rather to get an interview.
A resume should be a comprehensive picture of oneself, showing all aspects of education and	A resume need not tell everything about the person, but merely help the applicant avoid getting

(continued)

MYTH	FACT
complete work history and accomplishments.	rejected at key points in the weeding-out process.
A resume should highlight all one's strong points and major accomplishments.	In some cases, yes: in other cases, many of your client's strong points and best accomplishments may be either irrelevant for a position or may show the prospective employer he or she is "overqualified."
A resume is a chronological listing of all one's positions and specific job duties.	Although many resumes are chronologically ordered, this is only one of several popular formats. Other formats include the "functional" resume and the "qualifications brief," both of which may or may not present a job history in complete chronological order.
A good, accurately prepared resume can be submitted for a wide range of positions in allied fields.	With increasing specialization and opportunities for parallel career changes, more and more individuals benefit from "variant resumes"; several different formats and emphases for the individual's range of job skills and professional or personal characteristics.

(continued)

MYTH	FACT
The best time to prepare a resume is when one is looking for a new job.	This is the most common time, but not always the best. One should always have an updated resume on hand, just as one should have a valid driver's license even when one doesn't have a car available. You never know when some opportunity will come your way unexpectedly, and having an up-to-date resume available will make the difference between seizing an opportunity or letting it go by.

REMEMBER: The purpose of sending a cover letter is simply to get the person at the other end to read the resume. The purpose of a resume is to get a job interview.

In about 70% of the cases, there is virtually nothing of any substance to include in a cover letter; a sentence or two will do. Next to brevity, quality stationery and accurate typing and output are the best ways to assure that a cover letter will be noted.

There are several important exceptions to this. I have found that about 30% of the cases do require special material in their cover letters. These exceptions include situations . . .

- where some specialized skill, such as fluency in Serbo-Croation, is asked for and that single job skill can make the difference in getting the job.

- where the applicant is writing at the advice of someone who the reader will know or whose name will be positively recognized ("Joe Martino, your regional sales representative, suggested I write you . . ." or "Senator Bill Barkley thought you might be interested . . .").
- where circumstances prevent the applicant from listing something very relevant on the resume; something he or she wants the prospective employer to know about.
- where a resume must be directed toward the right person in an organization, especially in cases where a job title or category is ambiguous.

There may be other exceptions as well, but in general, the cover letter should do little more than state that a resume is enclosed for consideration of a specific position. It should not exceed 100 words.

The 5 Second Test

Studies have shown that the average resume is read – if that is the correct word – in less than 5 seconds! A personnel director or department manager who runs a classified ad in Sunday's paper will receive an average of 25-100 resumes a day, on Tuesday through Friday, and will hardly have the time to read any thoroughly.

So, you are probably asking, shouldn't there be something to catch the eye of the person reading it? Yes and no. Certainly, if a resume is prepared on iridescent pink paper, it will get special attention. But it is unlikely that such attention will result in anything more than a few chuckles and a pass around the office. Since the purpose of the resume is not to entertain, but to get an interview, this would hardly be a good idea.

However, there are ways of formatting a resume; highlighting it so that some quality, word, title, or phrase stands out above the others. For instance, the way you organize your material on the paper and set it up can highlight some points over others. Fancy letters that look printed can be created easily with Letraset letters, which can be neatly transferred on to the resume to make it look more impressive. From the master, the copies are then made on a fine bond paper.

A Simple Test

There is a simple test you can use to see what stands out in a resume. It will help you discover what the prospective employer will see when he or she quickly thumbs through a batch of resumes, one of which is your client's. This five-second test will help you format a resume in the most effective way, and show you the need for variant resume formatting.

Take a resume you are not familiar with and hold it up in front of you. Skim it casually for about five seconds as it would be skimmed by a prospective employer who has dozens of resumes on the desk. Or, better yet, take a few related resumes from your friends or from a resume book, and skim over the batch, allowing about five seconds for each. Now ask yourself what you remember about the resume(s). What stands out? The chances are that you remember something that falls into one of two categories: it appears in the center area, about 1/3 down the page; or the type is especially large or different from the rest of the page. This is the best way to determine what stands out on a resume you are preparing – and why.

The Resume "Hot Spot"

There is a certain area on every resume, especially on a one-page resume, which I call the resume hot spot. This hot spot stands out above all else on a quick reading, especially on a five-second text. It is located about 1/3 down the page in the center.

In preparing a resume, you can make use of this knowledge in two ways. You can include something especially important there, such as the fact that your client was graduated cum laude from Harvard or that her most recent position was vice-president at CBS. Another suggestion is to highlight some point about 2 inches to the right or left of the hot spot center, to which the reader's eye will be immediately guided.

Variant Resumes

Sometimes an individual is not sure what to emphasize on a resume; which aspects of his or her experience, education, or skills to highlight to their best advantage. Dr. Rose, for example, has held six different positions over the past ten years. These positions range from college professor to social agency head, to her most recent position as an employment consultant to the Ford Foundation. She is planning to send out approximately one hundred resumes; some to universities, some to consulting firms, some to public agencies, and some to private businesses where she hopes to obtain a position in the personnel field.

Although she is qualified for all these positions, each requires a different kind of emphasis. Thus, she is a perfect candidate for the variant resume; different versions emphasizing different aspects of her professional background and qualifications.

Skill Bank

To focus on the kind of resume that would be best for any individual client, to help assess whether to pursue variant formats or a single universal one, you should first audit the client's "skill bank." This term refers to all the skills and attributes – professional, technical, educational, and experiential – that he or she can offer to a prospective employer. These skills are the applicant's assets. One of the main jobs of the resume you are preparing is to enumerate these assets, giving each its appropriate emphasis.

As you and the client sit down to create this list, you may realize that the client possesses many skills not ordinarily used, or skills that have not been taxed in recent jobs. Tom Ciccone, for example, realized that his strong programming skills which were taken for granted in his present job, could be a valuable plus in other companies where there were not so many programmers. He emphasized this on one version of his resume, while leaving it as a minor point on another version, geared more for supervisory and sales/managerial positions. Bob Lieberman, worked for eighteen years as a hospital pharmacist in the "back room." He recognized that his positive personality traits and excellent interpersonal skills would have to be highlighted in the variant resume designed for a new position as pharmaceutical magazine advertising sales representative. Dealing effectively with advertising people and with medical professionals would be paramount for this position.

In tabulating your client's skill bank, you will typically find that some of the skills have been multiplying rapidly in value, earning dividends from the most recent positions. Other skills have been put aside, forgotten about for the time being, and may have to be reclaimed if they are to be made marketable. All this skill analysis should be done before you help your client prepare a resume. This will give you a firm idea of what the client has to offer before drawing up a qualifications prospectus.

Resume and Cover Letter Preparation

If you can develop the ability to prepare a professional-quality resume and cover letter, you can add substantial income to your word-processing business. You may wish to consult some of the excellent books available, such as Loretta Foxman's *Resumes That Work* or Burdette E. Bostwick's *Resume Writing,* both of which offer practical step-by-step advice in constructing good resumes that place your client in the best light.

Many clients will come to you with a poorly prepared resume and ask to have it typed. You can tactfully explain to them the faults with their present resume, using some that you have prepared to show why they are more effective. You can then offer to help fix their resume and, if they are wise, they will take you up on the offer.

Other clients will be attracted by advertising and word of mouth to your resume preparation services. By coupling the preparation skills with the word-processing services,you are helping them get a good resume out quickly. You are also relieving them of a burdensome and nonproductive anxiety that encumbers the task of preparing their own resume.

BUSINESS SUPPORT SERVICE

Another excellent source of potential revenues for your word-processing business involves specialized word processing and information management services for businesses: small businesses, larger corporations for which you will act as a "service bureau," and individual professionals and business people. As you develop a list of business clinetele, you will discover the specific kinds of services to offer. This section discusses a range of services that I have found to be most easily learned and readily sold.

What kinds of businesses can benefit from your services? Law firms and individual lawyers in private practice form a large group of clients. Unable to support a range of sophisticated word processing capabilities in their own offices, due to lack of trained staff or equipment, they can be easily shown how to use your services. They can save money and time in preparing documents, keeping client files, internal memoranda, and other functions (Figure 6.1). Hospitals and private doctor's offices, including group medical practices, can also prove to be a lucrative clientele. Once medical practitioners realize the highly inflated prices charged for most medical software – functionally identical to the database and accounting software that will run on your computer – they are likely to think twice before setting up their own systems. Hotels and convention organizations have a large volume of correspondence and public relations work. They can find many uses for your word processing service if you take the time to show them exactly what you can do an how it is cost effective for them. Most insurance offices require a range of ongoing word-processing services: record-keeping, sales/promotion and correspondence. You can also demonstrate to your local real estate offices how your business support services can improve their productivity and recordkeeping functions.

What kind of services can you provide? Your typing and letter/mailing list services, of course, are directly applicable in all these professions. In addition, you can choose from a range of powerful microcomputer/word-processor applications to sell your expertise to clients. All you need is the right software to run on your computer and the discipline to train yourself how to use it. The few examples that follow will give you an idea of what you can actually do.

Information Management

Most businesses rely on information. Accurate data is needed to set business goals, to realistically appraise the market, and to assess how well or how poorly the business is doing in relation to the current market. Product development, allocation of capital resources, advertising budgets,

ANALYSIS OF CALIFORNIA CONDO (PREPARED BY DAVID B. CONSULTANT)...PAGE 3

```
************** CASH FLOW ANALYSIS **************
                         %      1982      1983      1984      1985      1986      1987      1988      1989      1990      1991
                        ---    ------    ------    ------    ------    ------    ------    ------    ------    ------    ------
GROSS INCOME-
   ANNUAL RENTS          5     5,820     6,111     6,417     6,737     7,074     8,730     9,167     9,625    10,106    10,611

OPERATING EXPENSES-
   TAXES                 1     1,000     1,010     1,020     1,030     1,041     1,051     1,062     1,072     1,083     1,094
   OTHER EXPENSES        7     1,920     2,054     2,198     2,352     2,517     2,693     2,881     3,083     3,299     3,530
   *TOTAL OP'G EXPENSES 2.9    2,920     3,064     3,218     3,382     3,557     3,744     3,943     4,155     4,382     4,624

DEBT SERVICE-
   INTEREST            16    13,991    13,971    13,948    13,920    13,888    12,650    12,605    12,553    12,492    12,420
   PRINCIPAL           .13      115       135       159       186    10,218       256       301       353       414       486
   *TOTAL DEBT SERVICE 14    14,106    14,106    14,106    14,106    24,106    12,906    12,906    12,906    12,906    12,906

   *PRE-TAX CASH FLOW  -11   -11,206   -11,060   -10,908   -10,751   -20,589    -7,920    -7,683    -7,437    -7,182    -6,918

TAX CREDIT(OR LIAB) DUE TO-
   NET INCOME(LOSS)    50     5,546     5,462     5,375     5,283     5,185     3,832     3,691     3,542     3,384     3,216
   DEPRECIATION        50     3,638     3,032     2,727     2,423     2,122     1,822     1,822     1,822     1,822     1,522
   *TOTAL CREDITS(LIAB'S) 50  9,183     8,494     8,102     7,706     7,307     5,654     5,513     5,364     5,206     4,738

   *AFTER-TAX CASH FLOW -2   -2,023    -2,566    -2,806    -3,046   -13,282    -2,266    -2,170    -2,073    -1,976    -2,181


************** R-O-I ANALYSIS **************
                         %      1982      1983      1984      1985      1986      1987      1988      1989      1990      1991
                        ---    ------    ------    ------    ------    ------    ------    ------    ------    ------    ------
*GROSS SALES PRICE      10   110,000   121,000   133,100   146,410   161,051   177,156   194,872   214,359   235,795   259,374

SALE EXPENSES-
   COMMISSION           6     6,600     7,260     7,986     8,785     9,663    10,629    11,692    12,862    14,148    15,562
   ESCROW               1     1,100     1,210     1,331     1,464     1,611     1,772     1,949     2,144     2,358     2,594
   OTHER SELLING COSTS  2     2,200     2,420     2,662     2,928     3,221     3,543     3,897     4,287     4,716     5,187
   LOAN BALANCE              89,885    89,750    89,591    89,405    79,186    78,930    78,629    78,276    77,862    77,376
   TAXES ON GAINS       20    2,343     6,161     9,876    13,506    17,078    20,615    24,446    28,600    33,108    37,706
   *TOTAL SALE EXPENSES     102,127   106,801   111,446   116,088   110,759   115,490   120,614   126,168   132,191   138,426

CASH RETURN-
   NET EQUITY RETURN         7,873    14,199    21,654    30,322    50,292    61,667    74,258    88,191   103,603   120,949
   CUM CASH FLOW (FV)   5    -2,023    -4,690    -7,731   -11,163   -25,003   -28,520   -32,116   -35,794   -39,561   -43,719
   *TOTAL RETURN             5,849     9,509    13,924    19,159    25,289    33,147    42,142    52,396    64,043    77,230

CASH INVESTMENT-
   DOWN PAYMENT             10,500    10,500    10,500    10,500    10,500    10,500    10,500    10,500    10,500    10,500
   CUM CASH FLOW (PV)   5     1,927     4,254     6,678     9,184    19,591    21,282    22,824    24,227    25,501    26,840
   *TOTAL INVESTMENT         12,427    14,754    17,178    19,684    30,091    31,782    33,324    34,727    36,001    37,340

RETURN ON INVESTMENT (AFTER TAX)-
   TOTAL R-O-I (%)          -44.3%     -9.4%     32.6%     82.5%    140.9%    215.7%    301.4%    399.0%    509.9%    635.5%
   TOTAL I-R-R (%)          -44.3%     -4.8%      9.9%     16.2%     19.2%     21.1%     22.0%     22.3%     22.3%     22.1%
   EQUITY R-O-I (%)         -36.6%     -3.8%     26.1%     54.0%     67.1%     94.0%    122.8%    154.0%    187.8%    223.9%
   EQUITY I-R-R (%)         -36.6%     -1.9%      8.0%     11.4%     10.8%     11.7%     12.1%     12.4%     12.5%     12.5%
   RETURN ON EQUITY (%)       1.7%     47.8%     32.7%     26.0%     22.1%     18.1%     16.9%     16.0%     15.2%     14.6%
   CONVENTIONAL IRR (%)     -44.3%     -3.9%      9.1%     14.0%     16.0%     16.5%*    16.6%     16.5%     16.3%     16.1%
   F-M-R-R (%)              -36.6%     -1.9%      8.0%     11.4%     10.8%     11.7%     12.1%     12.4%     12.5%     12.5%
```

Figure 6.1 Your word processor can generate professional business reports and spreadsheets. This example was prepared on an IBM-PC, using Howardsoft's Real Estate Analyzer software.

and marketing strategies all depend on the continuing flow of accurate, up-to-date information.

While most large businesses have their own research staffs, the smaller business is often at a disadvantage in gathering and processing information. A toy manufacturer wants to know what regulations are being passed in different parts of the country regarding children's toys. An investment counselor is concerned about the economic forecasts for the Brazilian coffee economy. A gift shop owner needs to find a manufacturer of personalized pens. An independent stockbroker wants to get the most up-to-date, detailed information about several new bioresearch companies. A builder wants information about new solar heating devices.

You can provide most of this information right from your computer terminal by using what are called *online information services.* These electronic information banks send signals through ordinary phone lines which you, at your microcomputer or word processor, can capture on your floppy disks. You can then change and edit as you will, and print out the information for your clients in neat professional forms. Here is how it works.

When you want information, it can generally be found somewhere in the range of printed material that fills our libraries, including:

Books – technical, scholarly, professional reference
Periodicals – popular magazines, technical and professional journals
Government publications
Newspapers, serials, and special publications
Directories, telephone yellow pages, and business guides
Bibliographies, dictionaries
Encyclopedias, catalogues, indexes, registries

Finding the specific information to answer business questions requires a lot of specialized knowledge (where to look for what) and many hours of labor at libraries, which may not have all the works you need. To find the regulations governing children's toys, for example, you would want to search through government publications, law books, and probably trade journals for the toy business. To locate a manufacturer of personalized pens, you would use a phone directory or manufacturer's directory – but which is better? Economic forecasts of the Brazilian coffee economy would require reading pages of newspapers such as the Wall Street Journal, as well as government and trade publications. Prospects for investment in biomedical companies would involve understanding both the technology and the past stock performances. In all, this type of research is a lot of work.

Online searching can do in ten minutes what would take a day or more in the library, and takes a relatively short time to learn. All you have to do is dial up an online database service through your computer and code in your questions in a special format. There are several of these services, of which DIALOG™ is the most comprehensive. We will therefore use it as our example in showing how online searching works.

Each printed source (a book, a directory, an index, a volume of the Wall Street Journal) may be considered a database. A database, with respect to online searching, may be defined as a cluster of related information about a defined area. Using one or a combination of databases will allow you to gather current, accurate information for your clients. For instance, abstracts of all the articles published about solar heating may be located in one database, called *Energyline*. This database would enable you to inform your builder-client about everything available in that area, including books and journals, speeches, statistics, and congressional committee reports. Information for the stock-broker interested in bioresearch investment is available in three databases: *Medline*, which contains over 5 million entries about all aspects of medical and biological research; *Standard & Poors News,* which provides financial information on over 10,000 companies; *Claims,* which is a database of information about patents. The toy manufacturer's request can be thoroughly researched through three databases: *Trade and Industry Index,* which provides detailed information about everything appearing in toy journals or related to the toy manufacturing field; *UPI News,* which summarizes any news stories about the toy industry and federal regulations; *Legal Resources Index,* which specifically focuses on regulatory and legal issues related to the manfacturer's concerns. Once you learn the system of using databases, almost all the information in the world is at your fingertips.

Virtually all the major databases found in the library, even in the best business libraries, are currently available through interactive computer access, such as that provided by the DIALOG™ system. This means you can use your computer or word processor as a terminal, and call up the database, communicating with it through your keyboard. If you had to find each database separately, it would be almost as cumbersome as spending the day in the library – and just as old-fashioned. You can search many databases simultaneously through DIALOG™ in a matter of minutes, and have the information sent through the phone lines into your computer or mailed to you the next day.

Hooking up to DIALOG™ or a similar databank is really quite simple. Your word processor or microcomputer connects to the outside world through a modem (Figure 6.2). This piece of hardware translates your computer's electronic signals to impulses that travel over phone lines and return information the same way. Your computer or word processor also needs some special instructions about how to send and receive information through the modem. These instructions are contained in communications software, which may come with the modem or may be sold sepa-

Courtesy of Hayes Microcomputer Products, Inc.

Figure 6.2 A modem, which allows your computer to communicate over phone lines with other computers or with database systems, may be installed as a board. Pictured above, the Hayes Smartmodem 1200B can be installed in an IBM-PC, Compaq, Columbia, Corona, or other computers, requiring no additional desk space.

rately. A modem and the communications software costs around $300. You should check when purchasing a computer to find out if additional boards have to be installed in order to accomodate a modem.

The central computer to DIALOG™ is in California, but if you don't live in California, you can dial a local telephone number from one of the large electronic networking systems. Currently, there are three (Telenet, Tymnet, and Uninet) that have lines throughout the country and intersect with DIALOG™. When you become a DIALOG™ subscriber you get a code number that allows access to the system.

When I hook up to DIALOG™, I do the following:

1. Turn on my computer and modem and load the communications software.
2. Dial the local access telephone number, wait for a response prompt, and type my computer code.
3. Type the code to reach DIALOG™ and then enter my personal code which was given to me when I became a DIALOG™ subscriber. Now I am ready to search.

Searching

Once you are hooked into DIALOG, you have access to almost 200 databases, educational, scientific, and professional area. The strategy for searching any of these is provided in the documentation available when you become a member of DIALOG. Despite small differences, most searches follow a similar format.

The first thing you usually want to do is find out which databases to search. How do you know what information is in which database? DIALOG provides a simple device, called Dialindex™, which finds the right databases for you. Unless you know exactly where to look, you go to this database first and request the names of the databases that contain the information you need. In the following example, what you type in is indented and the DIALOG response is flush left. The material in brackets explains what the commands and responses mean:

```
Q.      b411 [Tells DIALOG you want to begin file 411, Dialindex]
R. File 411: DIAL INDEX (tm)
Q.      ? select files solar energy [asks DIALOG which databases
include information on solar energy]
R. File 8 COMPENDEX - 1978-83/DEC
R. File 69 ENERGY LINE
R. File 103 DOE ENERGY
R. File 169 ENERGYNET [DIALOG identifies the four files where the
information on solar energy is recorded]
Q.      ?solar energy (w) new homes [You are asking DIALOG to find
the entries that combine information about solar energy with new
home building].
R.      File        Items        Description
        ------------------------------------------------
        (8)            45        SOLAR
                      282        ENERGY
                       90        SOLAR(W)  ENERGY

        (69)          103        SOLAR
                      297        ENERGY
                       14        SOLAR(W)  ENERGY

        (103)         126        SOLAR
                     1558        ENERGY
                       92        SOLAR(W)  ENERGY

        (169)         561        SOLAR
                     3417        ENERGY
                      440        SOLAR(W)  ENERGY
```

If you are planning to use the DIALOG service, there is a two-day seminar offered in most cities that will train you on conducting database searches and storing all the information you gather in the memory of your computer. Learning this is not especially technical. It will allow you to increase significantly the capacity of your word processor or microcomputer by making it an online information terminal.

Research and Bibliographic Assistance

Just as you provide information to businesses, you can become a provider of information to individual clients who require research information for dissertations, corporate reports, term papers, books, or other works. In fact, much of the information you gather and store on your disks can be resold if your client base is broad enough to include many users with similar interests. For example, if you attract a clientele of independent insurance agents in your county, you will find that you can provide them with current information to keep them abreast of the market and to identify problem areas in regulations, sales patterns, and finance. One thorough search can be used over and over again. Likewise, if you attract college students writing term papers, a few key searches in each discipline becomes a reusable library of information that is not only resold, but attracts word processing typing jobs as well.

I usually charge between $200 and $500 for providing a complete list of abstracts for a person writing a dissertation or technical book. The work takes me about an hour and my expenses are between $70 and $200. The profit, as you can well see, is high. I charge $50 for providing enough information for a typical term paper. My costs are about $10 and it takes five to ten minutes of my time to do the search. For many students, this is a reasonable fee for saving a week of library time, and it also has some education value. I show them how I do the search and encourage them to learn this modern way of scholarship rather than the antiquated methods they have been using.

It is helpful, if you are going into this area of word processing, to keep careful records of where all your database information is stored. In a matter of months, you may have several disks of information and the problem of locating specific databases increases geometrically. I create a master cross-referenced catalogue that I update every time I add new information to my database. This allows me, in minutes, to determine if the information the client needs is already on my system, increasing my profit ratio to a full 100%.

Attracting clients for this type of service is a combination of word of mouth referrals and cleverly targeted advertising, including personalized letters generated on your word processor. I advertise regularly in all the college newspapers and send hundreds of letters to students enrolled in doctoral programs in the New York area. I bought the mailing list of student names for $300 and make excellent use of it.

Boilerplating

In addition to information and research services, boilerplating is another business related service. Boilerplating is the word processing technique of having key sections of a document, such as a contract, or will, on your system and being able to assemble them by keying in a few codes. For example, I do a lot of work for lawyers who prepare wills. Most wills are basically the same, with some fill-in information (name of beneficiary, executors, etc.) and a few special clauses for individuals in special situations.

When I have an attorney as a client, I prepare a disk with about 50 standard will clauses, submitted by the client. The client is given a master sheet, on which he or she fills in the names of the testator(rix), the executor and beneficiary, guardians, sums of money, and so forth. The lawyer then checks off the order in which the clauses will be put together. I then fill in this information, using the word processor's find and replace functions. For instance, all occurrences of %% are replaced by the name of the testator and all occurences of @@ are replaced by the name of the executor. I then select those paragraphs and have them printed and numbered in order. It usually takes about 20 minutes to get an entire will (8-10 pages) formatted and printed. I charge $2.00 per page, yielding a profit of about 50%. This, of course, is in addition to the original, one-time charge for having the material typed into the word processor.

Boilerplating is commonly used for such documents as legal contracts, real estate prospectus, medical and psychological reports and building inspection reports. I approached a real estate office that was active in the co-oping of buildings. I pointed out how their 200 page reports for each prospective co-op, which were prepared in-house and submitted to their lawyers (an odd arrangement, I admit), could be boilerplated. This would not only allow them to be run off more quickly, but would eliminate the delay when the lawyer suggested certain changes requiring retyping.

Another client was a psychiatric social worker who had to prepare specially formatted psychosocial reports for 4 or 5 clients per week. She previously had these individually typed. About 50% of each report was identical, with only a specific number or date filled in. The other 50% consisted of different kinds of information. By setting up a boilerplating model, I could save her 30% on her typing costs, while at the same time increasing my profit by 30%.

Teachers who have to prepare an Individualized Educational Plan for each of their students are potential clients for boilerplating. In fact, I have a disk in my library that consists of 200 behavioral objectives, from which the teacher can select the 10 or 20 that apply to each student and fill in the number that would pertain to that student. For example, one objective reads:

[NAME] will demonstrate an increase in reading level from _____to _____in [X] months.

The teacher faills in the blanks for the student and the machine automatically replaces all occurrences of [NAME] with the student's name.

Newsletters, Catalogues, and Brochures

Many businesses, social organizations, and educational institutions put out newsletters, catalogues, or brochures. These publications inform members and employees about policies, boost organizational morale, list courses and class schedules, communicate informally with customers or membership, or serve a public relations purpose. Schools, scout troops, camps, cooperative and condominium boards, professional training institutes and others use newsletters to increase their visibility and keep their friends and members informed.

A potentially lucrative area for your word processing business is in the typing and printing of these catalogues or newsletters. You can also, for an additional fee, fold and staple them and send them out. This service can be provided in several ways; in conjunction with an offset/copy service or professional printer, or primarily through your own word-processing business.

Assume that the client provides you with the copy, the written material, for the newsletter. If effective writing is among your skills, you may want to prepare the copy for newsletter production, in addition to providing word-processing service.

Your client's written copy is then input into the word processor and aligned in the format and style in which it is to be printed. This can be columnar format (if your word processor can deal efficiently with columns – not all can), set as justified or ragged text, or any other format desired. Special print faces can be used for headings and for emphasis.

To create special printing effects for reproduction, without the expense of typesetting equipment, you can use the LetraGraphix Typesetting System™ (Figure 6.3). This is

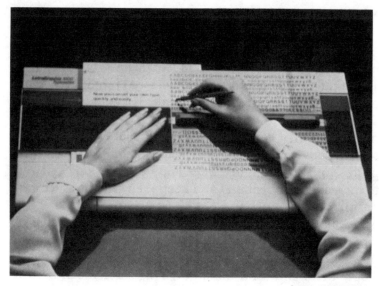

Courtesy of Letraset USA, Inc.

Figure 6.3 Resumes and business reports can be made more attractive with a letter transfer system, such as LetraGraphix.

a system of transfer letters, in a wide selection of fonts, colors, and styles. You rub off each letter with a burnisher – the pen-like tool that comes with the system. The letter is then transferred onto the paper and is suitable for a variety of types of reproductions. The system is inexpensive and gives a remarkable simulation of professionally typeset lettering.

Most stationery and art supply stores carry the LetraGraphix system or comparable letter transfer products.

If you produce a presentable master copy, generated on a daisy wheel or correspondence quality, dot-matrix printer, with transfer letters used for highlighting or for the title, this master copy can be brought to a photo-offset shop for reproduction. The cost of photo-offset is relatively low, but the cost of the paper and special ink colors can add substantially, especially if the client wants a professional looking product. For example, I produced a catalogue for a school. The cost was tabulated as follows:

Word processing cost	$70.00
Photo Offset (500 copies onfolded) 70 lb. bond	150.00
Folding and mailing (in addition to postage)	50.00
TOTAL:	$270.00

This averages 54 cents a catalogue, plus postage – a relatively high cost. My profit was $35 of the $70 for the word processing costs. Doubling the amount printed would leave my profit the same but increase the total cost by $100. The cost per catalogue would then be reduced to 37 cents ($370/1000).

I make much of my profit by helping write the newsletter or catalogue. For the job mentioned above, I helped write the course descriptions and the registration/admission procedures. For another job, I helped prepare a private school's newsletter. I interviewed some of the teachers briefly by phone, looked at notes and suggestions submitted by the staff, and threw in a few of my own bonbons for good luck. The work took two hours and I charged $75 as my fee – all profit. Not bad, is it? Of course, I used my writing skill to add to my word-processing business.

Newsletters, brochures, and catalogues can also be prepared by a phototypesetting procedure. Phototypesetting is a computerized photocomposition system that allows input from a keyboard similar to a typing keyboard. The computer regulates the spacing, allows justification, and can change the typestyles in a document. Offset methods require that you type your material on a word processor, then photograph the material and run it off. Photocomposition works directly from the keyboard. While the process is generally expensive, there is a big savings if you are using a word-processing system that is widely used. You can submit your disks to the photocompositor, who, with the appropriate software, can transform them into photo-offset plates. This saves the cost of rekeyboarding, and is highly cost effective.

WORD-PROCESSING TRAINING

The training of word-processing operators is a potentially lucrative area if you have the type of equipment on which the trainee will be able to find jobs. You must also have the personality characteristics and interpersonal skills required of a good teacher. You need patience, understanding of peoples' fears about computers, a willingness to spend a lot of time teaching, and all the other characteristics that make an effective teacher. If you meet these criteria, read on and I will show you how to make money without ever having to type again.

Most people who type want to learn word processing. They realize that typing is more repetitive and less interesting than word processing and that most word-processing operators make significantly more money than typists. But they are not able to learn word processing without buying a word processor or computer – an investment that would not be justified for a person looking for a salaried position.

I set up a word-processing program to train operators on Vydec and IBM word processors, and with WordStar™ software on a range of other equipment. I attract clients by advertising and by word of mouth. I counsel them realistically about job opportunities, test their skills on the machine, and train them to be word-processing operators. You must carefully check the laws of your state regarding educational training programs. In some states, you need a license if you claim to be a trainer; in some, you don't need a license as long as you don't claim you are a school. Some states define a school by the number of students trained; other states use different criteria. Find out the rules in your state to avoid the costs and embarrassment of charges of misrepresentation.

The first operators I trained were the people who were going to be working for me. I didn't get paid for that, of course, but I learned what goes into training and what qualities to look for in a potential trainee. Above all else, good typing is important; if your trainee can't type well, they will have difficulty getting a job, no matter how well the machine itself is mastered.

As I was training my own operators, their friends and family would call and offer to pay me to train them. How much to charge? Well, I knew by this time that it takes the average person 20 to 30 hours of hands-on experience at the machine. I didn't have to be with them every minute; in fact, I usually found that 10 minutes of instruction required 90 minutes of practice to master. So, I would personally spend about 4 hours of direct contact time with the trainee; the rest of the hours designated as student practice time. I also found that if I prepared some notes for the student to use, and some well constructed exercises, they didn't need me around too much and could get by on their own. Assuming that I purchased a word processor just for training, and the lease cost was $300 per month, if I had students working on it 80 hours per month (that's about four students), I could charge $5 per hour for training and make $100 profit a month and pay off my machine in a year. This, of course, is in addition to the money I made doing word processing at the same time.

Then, I made a remarkable discovery. When I went to investigate word-processing training in my area, I found that the schools were charging $15 per hour. If I were to charge only $12 per hour, undercutting them by 20%, I would still be clearing over $8 per hour real profit—in addition to the work I was doing on the machine. The idea began to seem quite sensible.

There were, of course, a few surprises. First, I found that advertising – not computer costs – were the most significant factor in my budget. Then, I found that selling the course to prospective clients – not teaching – was the most time-consuming part. Still, after a year, I was charging a flat fee of $295 for the course and making a lot of money.

The three stages of running a word-processing operator training program are: getting clients; training clients; placing and following up. Take a look at each.

Attracting clients

While word-of-mouth is an excellent way of attracting clients, it is slow. To build a training business, you will have to advertise. I have found the best place to advertise (in addition to the free advertising opportunities discussed in chapter 4) is in the classified or education section of your newspaper. This is where the career training and secretarial training schools have their ads. This is the section that will be read by your prospective clients. While advertising rates vary considerably, my advertising expenses were about $300 per month, which meant that my first student paid my advertising fee and the second student paid the computer lease cost. All additional students were profit, at a rate of $295 each. If I could sign up 5 students a month, I earned a profit of $885 per month in addition to paying off my computer with the earnings.

Your advertisement will probably be smaller and less spectacular than the training school ads. A typical ad may look like this:

WORD-PROCESSING TRAINING
If you can type you can learn word processing in 2 weeks. Full or part time training available. Complete course $295, including practice time. Call 763-2689 for free demonstration lesson.

Although this little ad will not stand out like the larger ones, a person reading this section of the paper to find out about skills training will generally notice the ad if it is run continuously. I have found that when I begin a new ad campaign, I run the same ad every Sunday or Wednesday, typically the days for these types of ads. A typical 8 week response pattern may occur like this:

First Sunday	2
Second Sunday	3
Third Sunday	2
Fourth Sunday	5
Fifth Sunday	9
Sixth Sunday	11
Seventh Sunday	14
Eighth Sunday	12

Notice that it takes a few weeks to get responses. The same person may look over the ad for a month or two before actually making the call for the free demonstration lesson. This is why it is especially important to advertise in the same paper, on the same day of the week, and in the same section. The person who remembers your ad will then be able to find it when he or she wants to begin the course.

If you are unsure of the best day of the week for your ad, just look for the secretarial or typing school ads in the paper or call the classified advertising department of the paper. They will tell you the best time to advertise and in which section. Don't make the mistake of trying the ad out for a couple of weeks and waiting to see what happens, or switching days. Consistency is the most important principle in attracting clients.

When the prospective trainee calls you in response to your ad, it is desirable to have him or her come in for a meeting. You can sell your course better and get a sense of whether this person will be right for the course only by meeting the person. About 90% of all my students were sold at the initial meeting, with the remaining 10% divided between those who enrolled by phone and those who required follow-up meetings.

At the initial meeting, you should test the applicant's typing skills and ability to comprehend simple instructions about how the machine works. People are often unusually nervous in front of a machine and this factor should be taken into account. Explain clearly what the course will entail, how you expect to be paid, and what you see as realistic job opportunities upon completion. I also suggest that the applicant call two of my graduates now working in the field to find out about the work and to see how well I provided the training.

Training Your Students

Much of your training design will be intuitive; dependent upon your teaching style and the nature of the equipment to be learned. I have found some general rules, however, that facilitate learning a word processing system.

I generally begin with input-typing exercises, which includes keyboarding, moving the cursor around the screen, and inserting/deleting material. I don't present every move at once, but begin with the simplest and most commonly used. I provide pages of interesting material to practice typing from. I have found that if the student enjoys reading the material, he or she is more likely to demonstrate the patience necessary for the task. It is also a good idea to begin with short documents, a page or less, so the student keeps a perspective of what he or she has done and where he or she is going.

After the basic moves are mastered, I move on to saving and retrieving material from the disk. I find that many students do not understand the relationship of computer memory and disk storage: they think that changes made on the screen are automatically made on the disk. I show them, through examples, the importance of saving documents and of keeping track of where the various drafts are stored.

Next we get into block copy techniques. I have them type an imaginary letter from Thomas Edison about inventing a word processor. Then, I have them move two paragraphs around a couple of times and, finally, delete a paragraph. We work on this until they get a sense of how blocks are handled by this word processor.

We then begin our final set of exercises using long documents (10 pages) that are already on the disk for them. These long documents are used for repagination, printing, and search and replace functions. I also use the long documents for the spelling checks. The final part of the course consists of the student typing in, editing, and printing a five-page single-spaced document.

Placing Your Graduates

Success in the word-processing training business is largely dependent on how well your graduates do in the job market. Your best advertisement is a student who learned in your course and is now out there earning $14 an hour for word processing. I make an effort, therefore, to help the student get a job upon completion of the course.

I don't act as an employment agent. On the contrary, I have established excellent relations with employment agencies who specialize in placing word-processing operators. These agents know that when I recommend a student who has completed my course, they are getting someone qualified for the job. And, because I know the kinds of tests that will be given at the agency and by the prospective employer, the student is rehearsed and trained to do well on these tests; a logical practice, since the tests accurately reflect performance.

SUMMING UP

This chapter surveyed a wide range of professional services that a word-processing business could offer. The guiding principle throughout has been to assess your individual talents, interests, and aptitudes to determine what aspect of the business is right for you.

Every word-processing business provides typing and printing services. That is usually the heart of the operation and pays the rent. But when you begin to look into the kinds of things you are typing and running off, you will find that you can offer the client more than he or she expects. That is how to go beyond word processing to build a business that reflects your personal skills and competencies.

7

Questions and Answers About Word Processing

Question. I have a new Apple IIe™ computer that I want to use for word processing. The computer is just as it comes, with a monitor and nothing else. I use a cassette tape for storage and have no software or disk drives at the present time. The salesman I went to for advice told me it would be cheaper to junk it and buy a complete new system that would be an excellent word processor. Is this good advice? Isn't there some way I can make my almost new Apple IIe into a word processor at less expense?

Answer. It is possible that the salesman is right – at least in terms of the lowest cost. Consider what you would need to upgrade your system into a workable word processor. You would have to buy two disk drives and disk controller card (about $700.00). You need an Apple 80 column card for any word processing applications (another $700.00). If you want a powerful word-processing program, you would need a CP/M® board with memory installed in your Apple (another $450.00). Finally, you have to buy the word processing software, with the mailing merge and spelling checker programs (about $600.00). So, to convert your new Apple into an excellent word processor would cost you about $1800.00.

For even less than that, you can buy a Morrow Decision or a Kaypro II™, which is set up and fully configured for word processing. When you buy a Kaypro or Morrow, the two disk drives, the 80-column capability, and the Wordstar (or an equivalent package), are included in the base price. As with your Apple, you would still have to add the printer. But the truth is that it is possible to start anew and spend less money than if you tried to upgrade your Apple IIe.

There is a cheaper solution however; one that will enable you to hold on to your Apple. With one disk drive and controller card ($400), you can purchase Applewriter® word-processing software ($175) and, despite its limitations, get going in your business. You would still need the 80 column card and printer, of course. So, for less than $700 (plus printer), you would have a fairly decent word processor—one that is certainly suitable for a start-up business.

Question. I have an IBM-XT® which I use for my business. I do financial planning from an office in my home. I am just building up my business and it does not yet generate enough income for me to pay for my machine and make a living. I thought I could make some additional money to cover my monthly lease payments by doing word processing in my spare time, but I don't type. Do you have any suggestions?

Answer. I have two suggestions. First, you can make money with your PC, even without typing, by renting out time on it. With a machine that is so widely used, you will find many individuals who know the machine from their offices, but need personal time to practice, to learn a program, or to do some personal typing. Even if you don't type, individuals can do their own word processing on your machine and you can show them how. In my area, machine rental time is $12 per hour, but it varies in different areas. If you can build up a clientele that will rent 15 hours per week, this will cover your lease payments in their entirety.

My second suggestion is to run a word-processing business by hiring typists and training them on your machine. Naturally, you won't make as much as if you typed yourself, but you should be able to cover much, if not all, of your lease payments. You might also consider buying a typing program, many of which are now available for the IBM-PC, and learning to type. This skill will help you in all aspects of your business.

Question. With so many different brands of computers on the market, and new ones being introduced each week, I'm totally confused about what to buy for my proposed word-processing plans. I want to spend no more than $4,000.00 for the whole system, but I've seen at least 15 different systems in that price range. Help!

Answer. Your problem can be simplified greatly by one simple rule: choose your word-processing software first and then look at the machine. You will find two main kinds of word processing software suitable for a professional word-processing business: those that run under CP/M® and those that run under MS-DOS (also called PC-DOS®). Forget the technical terms: what this means, in effect, is that if you buy a computer that works with CP/M or MS-DOS, you can purchase some good software. Once you've chosen your software, you look at the specific functions. For example, let's say you decide to go along with Wordstar™ – the most popular and, according to many, the best word-processing software available. Wordstar will run on both CP/M or MS-DOS, but you must buy a version that is specific to the one or the other. After deciding on Wordstar, you will see different advantages and disadvantages from one machine to another. Can you control the cursor keys with arrows or do you have to use control codes? Does the computer have function keys to speed up your work and will these function keys work with Wordstar? The same is true when you select your printer. You have to find out if the printer you want will be responsive to all the excellent features offered in a high quality word-processing program. So, the rule is to select the software you want and then find out which machine it will perform best on by asking for an actual demonstration in the store where you are planning to buy it.

Question. I have my own small word processing business which I run from home. Most of my business is sending out mass mailings. How can I learn to research mailing lists for my clients, many of whom are in specialized or very narrow fields? For instance, I have clients in community education, in truck equipment sales, in sales of scales, and in other odd fields. Are there mailing lists in these strange areas and how can I find them?

Answer. Yes, there are, and believe it or not, they are easy to find. For example, there is a yearbook of the National Scaleman's Association (I'm not kidding!) that lists over 2,000 people and small companies that design, repair or service scales. Your client in the field of community education will be surprised that you can prepare a specific mailing list from a directory called *People Helping People Help Themselves,* which is offered free for the asking from a nonprofit community education organization in Flint, Michigan. Your client in truck equipment sales can have a mailing list prepared from the membership roster of the National Truck Equipment Association.

How do you find out about all these? There is a directory called the *Directory of Directories,* which is found in most libraries. This large volume lists and summarizes thousands of directories in business, industry, labor, banking, real estate, law, government, public affairs, education and virtually every other field. It is indexed by subject matter, much of it quite specific. For example, if you are asked to prepare a mailing list for a person applying for a banking position in Chicago, you can find the Chicago Bank Directory on page 173, which will then lead you to a mailing list of over 1,000 people who could offer your client a job in Chicago banking. I find this directory extremely useful for gathering mailing list information, and it might be worth purchasing if preparing mailing lists is a substantial part of your business.

Question. I recently bought word processing software to use on my Apple II Plus Computer. The salesman assured me that it could do everything I needed to run my business, going over, step-by-step, the specifications on your sheet. As I've learned the system, I find it is pretty inadequate and can't do many of the things promised. The salesman keeps telling me it is my fault; I haven't learned the system well enough. Is there something I can do?

Answer. These specifications are listed in Chapters 2 and 3 of this publication. Unfortunately, your situation is not uncommon. It is likely that a salesperson won't know what a given software product can and cannot do, since it is beyond the scope of any one person to know the entire range of software on the market. That is why I suggest strongly that you get a personal recommendation from someone who has used the product over a period of time, or at least, that you read a review in a computer magazine or in a book like this one. Then insist on a hands-on demonstration on your kind of equipment with your own benchmark tests before making the purchase.

Many of us have gotten stuck with software that doesn't do what we expected it to. If you look in the documentation or guarantee card, however, you will probably find a clause that reads something like this: "The company specifically disclaims any implied warranties or merchantability or fitness for any particular purpose." What this means, in plain English, is that you have no guarantee that this software will perform the tasks you expected. In short, you have no recourse: once you buy your software, as long as it works at all, you are stuck with it.

Question. I recently took on another operator to work with me in my growing word-processing business. She lives about 40 miles from me and has different equipment (I have a Morrow computer and she has a new Texas Instruments Professional.) Is it possible for us to send material back and forth by phone? For instance, can she type a job and send it to my printer so that I can print it up and give it to the client?

Answer. Yes. The fact that you have different computers and different operating systems is not important. What you need is this: both of you need a modem and communications software, and you should both be using word-processing programs that can accept text files from another system. Wordstar™ is an example of this. You can then transfer your text files (stored on the disk and sent over the phone lines in what is called ASCII format) from one machine to another. After the receiving machine "captures" the text, the word processing software on the receiving machine can reconvert it into appropriate format. You then print it on the receiving machine's printer.

Question. In purchasing a system, I realize there are many trade-offs. My decision about a printer has been confused by all the sales pitches. Specifically, should I get a slow daisy wheel or fast dot-matrix, both of which are about the same price ($500)? I don't know what to do.

Answer. In general, a dot-matrix printer, even one with so-called "correspondence quality printing," is unsuitable for professional word-processing applications. Your clients will find such output unacceptable, except for drafts. So, you are pretty much limited to a daisy wheel printer. In terms of cost, the trade-off is always speed, since the output of cheap and expensive daisy wheels are the same. The least expensive prints about 12 cps (characters per second), while a fast one will print 50 cps. Among the least expensive and slowest printers are the Brother HR-15, the Smith-Corona TP-1 and the NEC-15LQ, all of which produce excellent print quality at between 12 and 15 characters per second. You have to access your time and priorities. If you, or someone else, can sit by the printer for several hours after inputting, editing and formatting all your jobs, then buy the cheapest one, since it will produce acceptable output. If you feel your business will be dependent upon fast output, invest in a faster daisy wheel printer. As your business grows, you can add a sheet feeder and print spooler, both of which will effectively increase your profit output about 60%, making it more competitive with the lesser quality dot-matrix printer.

Question. I bought a Compaq computer because I'm on the move a lot, but I find that it is too heavy to carry many places I go. Also, I would like to be able to do some work on the beach or in my backyard, but the Compaq has to be plugged in. I have seen ads for little lap-size computers that appear to be perfect for the settings in which I want to work? Do these small computers have any possibilities for word processing?

Answer. Yes, they do. The lap computers (also known as hand-held or briefcase-portable computers) are well suited for word processing – providing you have a larger computer, such as your Compaq, to send the information to. Although the lap computers have tiny screens (4 to 8 lines) and little memory (4K to 16K), they have been carefully designed to allow text editing, which can then be converted to word processing on your full-size computer. Here is how it works.

You type in your document on the lap computer. It can store it in memory or, if it is too long, on a cassette recorder. You can send it by phone or by an adapter right into the memory of your computer. There, as an ASCII file, it can be

There are several excellent lap computers available today. The Radio Shack Model 100 is probably the largest selling. It features an 8-line screen with a built-in text editor and a communications port for sending your material to another computer. It also has a port to connect to a cassette recorder for storing your documents. The NEC PC-8200 (which is bundled with a word-processing program), Epson HX-20, and Hewlett Packard HP-75 are other excellent lap computers.

Question. I was doing quite well in my word processing business, so I thought, until I went to my accountant to figure out my taxes. To my shock, I owed the government over two thousand dollars which, of course, I hadn't saved. My accountant said I needed more deductions to avoid this problem in the future. Any ideas?

Answer. Most of the individuals I know who started businesses ran into similar difficulties the first year. If you are used to a salaried income and have grown accustomed to receiving a refund check at the end of the year, then you probably don't realize how fast the money you are earning is accruing tax liabilities. Usually, one good jolt is enough to get you organized into keeping accurate records. But how do you know where you stand in the middle of the year? How do you know whether purchasing that new disk drive now will be advantageous from a tax point of view?

Luckily, for those who have microcomputers, there is excellent software available that can help you with your tax planning and point out the best ways for you to limit your tax liabilities. The *Tax Preparer* (Howard Software Services, 6713 Vista Del Mar, La Jolla, CA 92037) and *Financier Tax Series* (Financier, Inc., 2400 Computer Dr., Westboro, MA 01581) are two excellent programs. Both of these will enable you to plan tax strategies and multiple-case situations. You can determine the best policy for you to use during the year to avoid the big tax bite at the end. As your income begins to grow, you put into the programs all the relevant information and it shows you what your tax will be under a variety of circumstances. You then decide which circumstances will offer you the best tax advantage.

Appendix

Recommended Software and Complete Systems

This appendix includes recommended, complete word-processing systems, word-processing software to run on your computer, as well as other types of software that will help you make your microcomputer more productive and allow you to use your time more efficiently. Since new software products are always being introduced, there may be many new packages available that are not listed here. Omission from this list does not indicate poor program quality. The following have been evaluated and reviewed widely, and all of them are safe choices.

RECOMMENDED WORD-PROCESSING SOFTWARE

Listed alphabetically, all of the following systems are completely adequate for running a word-processing business. It would be difficult to choose a favorite among them. Price and compatability with your system should be major factors in your choice. For those of you considering systems not listed below, use the rating comparison chart on pages 00-00 to help you make your decision.

APPLEWRITER IIe   Apple IIe Computer
Apple Computer
20525 Mariani Avenue
Cupertino, CA 95014
(408) 996-1010

Overall system is very easy to learn and to use, with excellent documentation. Includes a Word Processing (programming) Language, called WPL, which enables you to expand and customize your word-processing abilities. Makes use of the apple function keys on IIe and offers a useful glossary feature, and fair find and replace functions. The software has some serious limitations, as well. You cannot adequately preview on screen what your printed page will look like. Block procedures are cumbersome and extremely limited (1024 characters). Difficult to overtype generally: you have to delete before putting in new text. Advanced and customized features, such as those created with WPL, very difficult to learn and to implement. No dictionary or indexing features. (Note: only the IIe version can be recommended at all.)

BENCHMARK   CP/M AND PC/DOS
Metasoft
711 E. Cottonwood, Suite E
Casa Grande, AZ 85222
(602) 836-6160

A powerful and versatile program, with many excellent and unusual features. An advanced glossary feature and a calculation mode are clear advantages for technical and statistical typing. The program is not easily integrated with major dictionary or indexing programs – a disadvantage. Toggling between the insert and overtype modes is cumbersome.

EASY WRITER 1.1, EASY WRITER II
IBM, TI PROFESSIONAL
Information Unlimited Software
281 Arlington Ave.
Berkeley, CA 94707

This is a comprehensive, fully-loaded word-processing program, featuring almost all important word-processing capabilities. Like many powerful programs, however, it is difficult to learn. Interfacing with many nonstandard printers traditionally has proven a problem and you must check to be sure that all the features work with your printer. Support of vendor is adequate only with special purchase of support contract (about $80 for a year).

EXECUTIVE SECRETARY   Apple II Plus, Apple IIe
Sof/Sys
4306 Upton Ave. S.
Minneapolis, MN 55410
   Much more than just a word processor, this is an entire office information management and document-production package. Combines many features of a filing system and modified database (record-keeping) program, which makes it suitable to a wide variety of tasks that require the integration of information into documents, letters, and reports. It also has many options for customized user extensibility. Although it is relatively difficult to set up and learn and, on the II Plus, requires a modification of your hardware which may void your warranty, it is tied with Format II as my all-around favorite word-processor for the Apple.

FORMAT II   Apple IIe, Franklin
Kensington Microware Ltd.
919 Third Avenue
New York, NY 10022
   If you are going to use an Apple or Franklin, this might be the software for you. Better than Applewriter, but with a few limitations that make it cumbersome, Format II is a powerful word-processing system that allows a wider range of print formatting than does Applewriter and has capabilities for merging other text files.

MULTIMATE   IBM and compatibles
Soft Word Systems, Inc.
52 Oakland Ave. North
East Hartford, CT 06108
   This package is derived from the much-praised Wang dedicated word-processing system. Excellent support with toll-free hot line service and good documentation make this package a natural for those who have some fear of mastering the complexities of software like Wordstar or Perfect Writer. Among its best (and most unique) features are good column handling, easy editing, many single-key-stroke commands, and easy formatting of tabs and margins. Some of the functions perform slowly, but this is a relatively minor disadvantage for most word-processing applications. MultiMate would be

rated among the better word-processing programs for the IBM and compatibles.

NDM Software   Vydec Word Processors
New Dawn Micro
390 Main Street
Manchester, CT 06040
   The powerful series of enhancement programs available from NDM for Vydec dedicated word processors (1800 series) make this old workhorse of word processing a formidable competitor for all of today's word-processing applications. A powerful spelling checker, print formatting program, and column/block move utility, combined with the 64-line screen of the Vydec, offers word-processing power unsurpassed on any microcomputer, as of this writing.

NEC Word Processing
NEC Electronics
1401 Estes Ave.
Elk Grove, IL 60007
   This is a word-processing package designed specifically for the NEC computers. It does an excellent job in all areas, and there is no reason to use any of the optional, board-based word processors, since this one will meet all your word-processing business requirements.

NORTH WORD   North Star
North Star Computers
14440 Catalina St.
San Leandro, CA 94577
   This is a word-processing package designed specifically for the North Star computer. It is excellent, and there is no reason to use any of the optional, board-based word processors, since this one will meet all your business requirements.

PEACHTEXT   IBM
Peachtree Software
3445 Peachtree Rd.
Atlanta, GA 30326
   A highly complex program with excellent long-document capabilities, including the merging of smaller documents into larger ones. An integrated spelling checker is available at additional cost, along with good telecommunications and mailing list programs. Much of the versatility of this software is for professional program-

mers who can use it to edit their programs, but it is comprehensive enough to be complete for a word-processing business.

PERFECT WRITER (IBM, CP/M Computers)
Perfect Software
1400 Shattuck Ave.
Berkeley, CA 94709

An old standby, Perfect Writer has many of the features of Wordstar, but not all. It is reasonably complex to learn, but fully utilizable for a word-processing business. It outshines Wordstar and other programs with its automatic footnoting capabilities, especially useful for typing dissertations. Not all features can be made to work with all printers. Because it comes bundled with many popular microcomputers (Kaypro, Columbia, Morrow, and others) it has enjoyed a wide popularity.

SCRIPSIT, SUPERSCRIPSIT TRS
Radio Shack-Tandy
1800 One Tandy Center
Ft. Worth, TX 76102

If you are one of the tens of thousands using a Radio Shack computer, there is not a great deal of high-level word-processing packages available. Fortunately, the SCRIPSIT programs, which are marketed by Radio Shack, are quite good and fully satisfactory for word-processing business applications. The upgraded and enhanced SuperSCRIPSIT compares favorably with CP/M-based packages, offering a range of features that will meet all your word-processing needs.

WORD PERFECT, version 2.24-L
IBM-PC and Compaq
Satellite Software International
288 West Center St.
Orem, UT 84057

A highly flexible and fully comprehensive word-processing system, suitable for the complex demands of a word-processing business. Its footnoting, columnar capabilities, and equation-writing formats are useful for a diverse range of documents. Disadvantages are that it is very complicated to learn and somewhat difficult to use. Also, it does not work completely with all printers so you should check first to see if it will support the capabilities of your printer.

WORDPLUS-PC   IBM, Compaq, TI Professional
Professional Software
51 Freeman Street
Needham, MA 02194

Based on a program written for a dedicated word processor, this software is a powerful, fully-functioning program that meets all the requirements of a word-processing business. Somewhat easier to learn than Wordstar, it is about as powerful. Because it is not nearly as widely used as Wordstar, you will not find as many references to it in books or as many knowledgeable individuals who can help out in a jam. On the whole, a fine system.

WORDSTAR, version 3.3
CP/M, IBM and compatibles, TI Professional, Apple, Franklin
Micropro International
33 San Pablo Ave.
San Rafael, CA 94903

The state-of-the-art, industry standard word-processing program. Runs beautifully on IBM-PC machines and compatibles, on all CP/M-type computers and on Apples with CP/M cards installed. Although it is a difficult program to learn, its versatility and scope make it an ideal word processor. Used in conjunction with Spellstar, Mailmerge and Starindex (sold as a "Professional Package" with the Wordstar program), this is a great word-processing package, although Spellstar leaves much to be desired as a spelling checker. I suggest you use Microspell (see below) with Wordstar for the ultimate combination.

You must be careful about the printer you choose. Only certain printers are included on the Wordstar installation menu. Although you can use another printer, it requires what is called a "custom installation," which is no easy matter unless you understand hexidecimal programming code. Look through the installation menu to see which printers are currently supported.

RECOMMENDED
ADDITIONAL SOFTWARE

In addition to your word-processing software, you will want additional software for checking spelling, mailing list applications, keeping financial records for yourself and your clients, graphics, telecommunications, improving the use of your computer memory, and so forth. While your specific decision about additional software will be based on what packages are compatible with the word-processing software you are using, I want to recommend a few packages I find especially useful. Before purchasing any of these, however, check to be sure that they will run on your system and with your present software. They are not really cost effective if they cannot integrate with what you are already using.

ELECTRIC WEBSTER (Proofreading program)
Cornucopia Software
P.O. Box 5028
Walnut Creek, CA 94596
More than just a spelling checker, this program, which should work with most of the recommended word-processing packages, also checks your grammar, offers suggestions, and assists with hyphenation decisions. For those writing to a specific audience, Electric Webster offers an analysis of readability and of sentence length.

MICROSPELL   CP/M, IBM, Compatibles
Trigram Systems
3 Bayard Road, #66
Pittsburgh, PA 15213
This is the best spelling checker I have tested so far. Works with any word-processing program that stores its files in ASCII format. Runs fast and offers intelligent guesses for the word you've misspelled. Corrects automatically at the touch of a key. Based on a model of artificial intelligence, this is a "smart" program that eliminates many of the unneccessary steps in many popular spelling checkers. Highly recommended.

THINK TANK (an idea organizing program)
Living Videotext
450 San Antonia
Palo Alto, CA 94306
If part of your word-processing business is writing letters or resumes for clients, this program might be for you. An unusual application, ThinkTank is designed to help you organize your ideas and reformulate them for writing. You can move around ideas, see how they work in different places, and "capture" your ideas in the word-processing program. ThinkTank will help you develop an outline for a letter, report, resume, or anything else that requires structured, logical thinking.

CACHE/Q
Techne Software Corp.
3685 Mt. Diablo Blvd., Suite 210
Lafayette, CA 94549
(415) 238-6824

No matter how much memory you have installed in your computer it is likely that only part of it is being used by your word-processing program. Have you noticed how different commands require the disk to be read over and over, or how the memory does not seem to be able to hold a long document? That's because the programs are written for the smallest possible memory so they will have a wide application. Cache/Q allows you to use all of your memory. For example, you can load your entire word-processing program into memory and remove the disk, allowing almost instantaneous access to all the commands without having to sit through the disk-access procedures. This will speed up your word processing considerably.

RECOMMENDED COMPLETE SYSTEMS

The prices of computers and, to some degree, of software, are always changing – usually dramatically downward. By the time you read this, you will probably find that many of these systems are available for less than the prices quoted here. These are six systems, ranging in price from $2000 to $6500, that I can personally recommend. Each gives you top value for the money spent.

I hasten to point out to those who are considering other systems, that many computers and printers not mentioned here may be just as good as these – or even better. They are not included simply because I am not familiar with them. The Apple IIe computer, with which I am familiar, is not a recommended machine for word-processing applications since it is neither cost effective (by the time it is enhanced to be suitable for a word-processing business) nor does it have a particularly good keyboard for extensive typing. However, for Apple and Franklin owners, there is some good software available, such as Executive Secretary and Format II (see the first section of this Appendix). All of the software mentioned in the following list is reviewed in the previous section.

KAYPRO (approx. $2000 – a best buy!)
Kaypro 2 or Kaypro 4 (add $400 to the system price)
Software included: Perfect Writer and Wordstar
Silver-Reed or Juki Daisy Wheel Printer

MORROW DECISION (approx. $2300 – a best buy!)
Morrow Decision with two disk drives, 64K
Software included: Perfect Writer or Wordstar
Silver-Reed or Juki Daisy Wheel Printer

VYDEC 1800 Dedicated Word Processor (approx. $3200)
Rconditioned Vydec 1800 with Qume printer included
Recommended Software: NDM (New Dawn Micro) Package:
Text Print, Dictionary, Versa Move

RADIO SHACK (approx. $3200, including printer)
Radio Shack TRS-80 64K Model 4 with 2 disk drives
Recommended Software: Scripsit or Superscripsit
Radio Shack Daisy Wheel II Printer

COLUMBIA or CORONA (approx. $4100)
Columbia or Corona Computer (desk top or portable),   128K,
2 drives
Software included: Perfect Writer or Wordstar
Qume Sprint printer

DECMATE (approx. $4800)
Decmate dedicated word processor with word-processing software and printer included. This is a top of the line unit with a
price to match, but a good value for the money. Reconditioned
units sometimes available.

Appendix

Glossary of Word-Processing Terms

Access time: The time, generally measured in microseconds, it takes for one part of a computer or word processor to receive or send data to or from another part. Typically, the time it takes to get information from a disk requires the longest access time, with a hard disk having a much shorter access time than a floppy disk. The fastest access time is from memory to the screen.

Acoustic coupler: An older type of modem in which the phone head set is actually cradled on the rubber cups of the transmitting device.

Alphanumeric: Refers to the collection of all the alphabetic characters (a,b,c,d. . .), punctuations and special symbols (.,?,",&,@. . . .), and numbers (1,2,3. . .).

ASCII: Stands for "American Standard Code for Information Interchange." Every alphanumeric character or special symbol is assigned a unique ASCII number between 0 and 255. These numbers are universally understood by all computers.

Automatic hyphenation: The ability to divide words at the ends of lines and automatically insert hyphens in the correct place or remove them when line lengths are readjusted.

Automatic Pagination/Repagination: The ability of a word-processing program to format pages to specific lengths (54 lines long, for example) and then, after editing, to be able to change pages to conform to the next text.

BASIC: The most popular programming language. Stands for "Beginner's All Purpose Symbolic Instruction Code."

Baud: Describes the rate at which bits of data can be sent from one computer to another over telephone lines or from one part of the system to another. Usually, the baud rate equals the number of bits per second that can be transmitted. There are two generally accepted telecommunication standards: 300 baud or 1200 baud (300 or 1200 bits per second, respectively).

Bidirectional printing: Refers to a printer that can print lines from left to right or from right to left. This type of printer is generally faster than a unidirectional one, especially where multiple passes of the print head are required for boldface or correspondence-quality printing.

Binary: Refers to the basic language of any computer or word-processing system. A binary number system is made up of zeros and ones only, combinations of which (0111010010110010), in groups of eight or sixteen bits, make up the "words" and "addresses" the computer understands.

Bit: The smallest unit of computer language, expressed as a 1 or 0, meaning that a switch is open or closed inside the computer circuitry.

Bits per Second: Also known as bps, refers to the speed at which information is moved within or between a computer system or systems.

Block: Refers to any chunk of text defined by the operator as a unit. May be a paragraph, part of a paragraph, several paragraphs, or any unit that is to be considered as a whole.

Block Indenting: In word processing, the ability to indent an entire paragraph or block (such as a quotation) by giving a command at the beginning to start the indentation and a command at the end to go back to the normal margins.

Block Move: The ability, in a word-processing program, to identify (mark) and move an entire block of text (one or several paragraphs, a half-page, a page, etc.) from one part of the document to another.

Boilerplating: The word-processing technique of creating and storing commonly used paragraphs, blocks, or sections of a document and assembling them to produce the final document. Commonly used in the legal profession for the creation of wills and contracts.

Bold Strike: A printing technique in which some letters, words, or phrases appear darker because the printer strikes over them several times. The ability to bold strike depends on the word-processing software and the printer capabilities.

BPS: *See Bits per Second and Baud.*

Bubble Memory: A new type of computer memory in which large amounts of operator-input information can be stored, even when the computer is turned off.

Buffer: An area of memory, either in the computer or in some peripheral (the printer or a spooler device), that temporarily holds information when it is transmitted faster than it can be processed. For example, when you give the command to print a document, the text can be sent to the printer much faster than it can be printed. The buffer can hold the text until the printer catches up to it, thereby freeing the computer memory while the printer is working.

Byte: Eight binary bits of information (11000110 for example) that are grouped together as a single word in the language of the computer.

Cathode Ray Tube (CRT): The display, screen, or monitor of the word-processing system.

Center Justification: The ability to center text automatically with respect to the currently set margins.

Centering: The ability to center text automatically with respect to the currently set margins.

Central Processing Unit (CPU): The part of the computer or word-processing system that actually processes the information. Usually consists of a small chip (the processor), memory chips and circuits, and various other circuits, (the data bus and input-output bus) that lead into and out from the processor and memory.

Chaining: The ability within the word-processing system to chain together files to form a longer document. Boilerplating is a form of chaining, usually with smaller blocks of material. *See Boilerplating.*

Character: In word processing, refers to any letter of the alphabet, any single-digit number, any punctuation mark or any special symbol (*s⅔⅝, etc.).

Chip: The tiny silicon processors or memory units inside the computer.

Column Moving: The ability to recognize and move vertical columns of material in a document, such as a column on a financial statement. Many word-processing systems are unable to deal well with columnar material.

Compatibility: Refers to the presumed ability of one word-processing or microcomputer system to use the software and hardware of another system, including the ability to work with documents created on one system and edit them on the compatible system. Compatibility is rarely 100%, and most compatibility is limited in certain types of operations.

Correspondence Quality Printing: A term generally used to describe a print quality better than normal dot-matrix, but not quite as good as letter quality.

CPI: Characters per horizontal inch. Refers to the "pitch" of the typed line, usually 10 or 12 characters per inch.

CP/M: The most popular microcomputer operating system, especially in the business and word-processing fields. Stands for "Control Program/Microcomputer." Different versions and variants exist, such as CP/M-86 and MP/M.

CPS: Characters per second. Usually refers to printer speed.

CPU: *See Central Processing Unit.*

CRT: *See Cathode Ray Tube.*

Daisy Wheel Printer: A letter-quality printer in which a plastic or metal wheel spins around, the spokes of which are struck by a solenoid hammer when the correct character is in position. Presently, this is the most popular type of printer for word-processing applications.

Data Communication: The sending or receiving of electronic data, usually over the telephone lines.

Database Management System: A computerized filing and recordkeeping system in which formatted records can be created and filled out; information retrieved, combined, or processed according to the specified criteria.

Data Processing: As differentiated from word processing, the processing of non-textual information, usually numeric. In data processing, the information is grouped into individual records, each of which contain several fields.

Dedicated Word Processor: A special computer built for word-processing applications. Usually includes special editing keys and buttons for printing and other word-processing operations. What are normally considered peripherals in a computer system (printer, disk drives, etc.) are all integrated as a part of the system. The word-processing software is included in the system. Many dedicated word processors can also function as microcomputers, sometimes with a special option that enables them to read popular software formats, such as CP/M.

Descending Characters: Refers to the ability of a dot-matrix printer to print characters such as "g", "y" and "p" with their tails below the line, as they appear here.

Deletion: The removal of characters, words, lines, sentences, paragraphs, blocks, or files.

Dictation/Transcription Equipment: A machine that can record dictation, either directly into a microphone or over the phone lines, and can then be used for transcription: it has the conveniences of cue/review, pause, speed control, etc.

Dictionary Feature: An option for many word-processing programs in which spelling is checked against a disk-based dictionary. *See Spelling Checker.*

Disk Drive: The most popular storage device in word processing. The drive spins a disk around and a read/write head picks up the magnetic information and transmits it to the computer memory or printer.

Disk Operating System (DOS): The main program of a computer or word processor. Enables all the parts of the system to function together and does all the system "housekeeping." Popular microcomputer disk operating systems include CP/M, PC-DOS, MS-DOS, TRS-DOS, and Apple DOS. Many dedicated word processors have their own unique disk operating systems and cannot run software written for other systems.

Diskettes: Flexible plastic disks in jackets which store the magnetic information from a computer or word-processing system. Also called floppy disks, popular sizes are the 5.25 in. or 8 in. formats, with the new 3 in. format beginning to emerge as an important new standard.

Disks: May be the same as diskettes or may refer to hard disks which are larger and store much more information than floppy disks. Hard disks are housed permanently in their drives and cannot be removed by the user. *See Diskette.*

Display: Another term for the screen, monitor, or CRT.

Distributed Word Processing: A system in which several terminals share a central processing unit and one, or several, printers. Applicable mostly to large office environments.

Documentation: The instruction (training) and reference manual that comes with a computer, word processor, peripheral, or software. Generally considered very important in making a purchase decision, since it enables the user to get the full value of the system.

DOS: *See Disk Operating System.*

Dot Matrix Printer: A fast, reliable, popular type of printer in which characters are formed out of tiny dots. Print quality varies from high-speed draft printing to specialized printing techniques where the dots are spaced so closely together that they appear to be typewriter quality.

Double Strike: A popular printing technique where characters are printed twice, one on top of the other, or very slightly misaligned. Produces darker, bolder, or more clearly defined lines of text.

Dual Pitch: Refers to a printer or typewriter than can be switched from one print size to another.

EBCDIC: *See Extended Binary Coded Decimal Internal Code.*

Elite: The older term for what is now more commonly called 12 pitch (12 characters per inch) printing.

Executive Interface: The functional contact between the manager or executive who is generating the information and the computer system on which the information is being written, edited, or processed.

Extended Binary Coded Decimal Internal Code (EBCDIC): A universally used coding system for representing data or words in a computer's memory or peripheral devices.

Facsimile (FAX): Refers to a machine that transmits or a method of transmitting images of printed or graphic material electronically from one place to another. In general, a method of photocopying where the original is in one location and the copy is produced in another.

File: Refers to any document or set of instructions stored on a floppy disk. The word-processing program itself may be a file or several files and each document or page you create may be stored as a separate file. Every file must have a unique name to distinguish it from other files on the disk.

File Control: The ability to mark, locate, save, retrieve, delete, and merge files.

Flagging: Refers to placing special characters or a sequence of characters (typically @, !!, or a period at the left-hand margin) in a text document to indicate a special situation, such as an index entry, a misspelling, etc.

Floppy Disks: *See Diskettes.*

Footers: Material included at the bottom of the printed page. Usually refers to vertical spacing (bottom margin) and page numbering.

Footnoting: In word processing, the ability to automatically include footnotes on the appropriate page. Also, the ability to keep track of footnote numbers and change them as text is moved around.

Form Letters: Correspondence that is being sent to several different people. In word processing, the ability to be able to automatically insert names, addresses, and other information into each letter, then print it.

Forms: A document type consisting of fields, each of which has constant information and a variable zone to be filled out (such as LAST NAME   ). Some word-processing systems are able to keep the variable information separately and fill out the form in the correct places.

Forms Tractor: A device that hooks up to the printer and allows sprocket-holed tractor paper to be fed through. Useful for unattended, automatic printing of long documents or multiple form letters.

Full Duplex: Refers to a method of transmitting information electronically which allows simultaneous transmission in either direction. An alternative to half duplex.

Global Search: The ability to automatically search through a document and locate a specific occurrence or occurences for which the user is looking. For example, you may want to look through a long document and quickly locate a name that occurs one or several times.

Glossary: In word processing, the ability to create special one or two-keystroke codes that will generate frequently recurring names, phrases, etc. For example, in a long book on biology, the > sign may be used to generate the phrase "phylogenetic factors and influences" every time it is pressed.

Graphics: The ability of a computer, using the appropriate software, to transform data and other information into visual presentation, such as bar and pie charts, diagrams, etc.

Half Duplex: A method of transmitting information electronically which allows transmission only one way at a time, as opposed to full duplex.

Hands On: Refers to learning or using a system while directly interacting with it.

Hard Copy: The actual printed copy of a document, as opposed to a disk file of the document.

Hard Disks: *See Disks.*

Hardware: The physical parts of the computer system, including its inner circuitry, as opposed to "software" which is the set of instructions that make the computer perform.

Headers: In printing, refers to the top of a printed page and the information included. Headers may include vertical spacing (top margin), titles, and page numbers.

Horizontal Scroll: The ability to create and view material wider than the word processor's or computer's screen. Useful for creating charts and tables that are more than the typical 80-character width word processors offer.

Hyphenation: The dividing of words at the end of the line. Some word-processing software offers automatic hyphenation that divides words in their appropriate places.

I/O port: Part of the central processing unit, to and from which information can be sent in and out. Generally classified as either serial ports, where information is transmitted one bit after another, or parallel ports, in which several bits of information are transmitted simultaneously. Most printers use the parallel port, while modems for telecommunications use the serial port.

Indexing: An option with some word processors in which an index of key words or concepts can be created from embedded commands in a document. Especially useful in locating information in a long document.

Information Processing: The general term that includes both data processing and word processing.

Ink Jet Printing: A fast and generally high-quality printing technique in which ink is sprayed through an electrostatic grid to form the characters on the paper.

Intelligent Printer: A term used to describe a printer that has a microprocessor inside which is capable of being programmed to perform special functions or applications.

Interface: Any connecting device or socket to hook up the parts of a computer system or one system with another.

Justification: The ability to line text up evenly at the left margin (left justification), right margin (right justification), both margins (full justification), or centered with respect to the margins (center justification). Text which is not justified is sometimes referred to as "ragged."

K: A kilobyte, or a thousand bytes of information. Used as a measure of memory or disk capacity.

Left Justification: The lining up evenly of the left side of each printed line of text.

LPM: Lines per minute; used as a measure of a printer's speed.

Machine Language: The binary computer code consisting of ones and zeros which is the basic language of all computers and word processors.

Magnetic Media: The media on which the files and software are stored as magnetic signals. Cassettes and disks are magnetic media, the latter being the most commonly used in word-processing applications.

Mail Merge: In word processing, refers to the ability to take information from a mailing list and merge it with documents or form letters.

Mailing Lists: Lists of names, addresses, and other pertinent information that can be merged with word-processing documents.

Mainframe: Refers to the large companies as opposed to the mini-computers and microcomputers. Many word processors or micro-computers have the ability to send or receive information from a mainframe over the telecommunication lines.

Mass Storage: Refers to the ability to store large amounts of information, such as on a hard disk which may store up to 10 million bytes.

Memory: The computer's ability to hold information at a single time. Volatile memory means that the memory disappears when the computer is turned off. Random access memory (RAM) is memory that you can write to or read from, changing it as desired. Read only memory (ROM) remains the same even when the computer is turned off, but it cannot be changed by the user. Memory is measured in kilobytes, with most word-processing computers having 64 kilobytes or 128 kilobytes of random access memory.

Menu: A technique used in many word-processing programs in which the computer presents a series of options to the operator (1–PRINT, 2–SAVE FILE, 3–DELETE FILE, etc.). The operator, by responding to the options, is able to activate certain functions or programs.

Microprocessor: The tiny silicon chip inside the computer, through which all of the processing is done.

Mini-Disks: The 3″ floppy disks introduced for microcomputer storage. Recently making some impact in the market with the introduction of the Apple Macintosh.

Modem: A device that attaches to a computer or word processor and allows information to be sent or received over regular telephone lines to or from other computers.

Operating System: *See Disk Operating System.*

Overprinting: *See Double Strike.*

Overtype: The ability to type over a letter or character. Especially useful in printing special symbols not available on the keyboard, including the cents sign, pound sterling sign, etc. *See also Double Strike.*

Page Display: The ability of a word processor (or of word-processing software) to show on the screen what the actual printed page will look like.

Page Numbering: The ability to automatically number pages of a multiple-page document, beginning with a page number the user requests and numbering in a format specified by the user (centered, right numbering, 1-2, 1-3, -4-, /5/, etc.).

Pagination: Also called repagination. The ability to automatically create new pages as text is added or deleted, or as the size specifications (margins, type size, number of vertical lines, etc.) for the printout are changed.

Parallel Interface: A connection between the computer and a peripheral device, such as the printer, in which several bits of information are transmitted simultaneously. Alternative to serial interface in which information is transmitted one bit at a time.

Pica: The older name for 10-pitch (10 characters per inch) printing.

Platen: The roller in the printer that the paper rests against as the letters are imprinted on it.

Print Wheel: In daisy wheel printers, the 4", spoked plastic or metal wheel containing all the printable characters. The print wheel can be changed for different type styles, special alphabets or symbols (Greek or scientific notation), or different pitches. *See also Daisy Wheel.*

Printing Functions: A general term to describe a word-processing system's versatility. Special printing functions include double striking, underlining, overtyping, compressed or expanded letters, super and subscripts, justification, etc.

Program: A series of instructions written to specifications that the computer can understand. A program may be written in a standard computer language such as BASIC or Pascal, or a special word-processing language, such as WPL which comes with Applewriter. A program you use to perform your regular word-processing or data processing functions is called an application program. A program that helps your computer do things more effectively (such as alphabetize your directory or allow you access to the inner workings of the system) is called a utility program.

Proportional Spacing: In printing, the ability to allow each character space that is consistent with its width; that is, allowing an "m" three times the space allotted to an "i." Proportional spacing produces nicer looking output. It is a function of the software and the hardware, both of which must support it for it to work.

RAM: Random access memory. The memory in the computer that you can read from or write to. Alternative to ROM (read only memory).

Random Access Memory: *See RAM.*

Read Only Memory: *See ROM.*

Read/Write Head: The small arm in the disk drive that reads data off the disk or writes data onto it. The read/write head mechanically moves to the track of the disk where the requested data is to be saved or retrieved, and is generally considered the slowest part of the disk storage system.

Records Management: Also called database management, a method of cataloguing and retrieving, in desired order, large amounts of information which are stored on the floppy disk and processed through the computer.

Repagination: *See Pagination.*

Right Justification: The ability to line up all the right ends of the lines evenly on a printout. Right justification is a combined function of the software and the printer.

ROM: Read only memory. The memory that comes on chips installed in the computer, from which you can read information but to which you cannot write (or change). Many computers include the BASIC programming language in ROM. Read only memory becomes available to the operator as soon as the computer is turned on.

Screen-Oriented: Used to describe word-processing programs that show, on the screen exactly, what the printed page will look like (including underlines, justified margins, etc.)

Search and Replace: The ability of a word-processing program to find occurrences of a character string and replace it as specified. For instance, if "Mr. Deluga" was accidentally misspelled "Mrs. Dluga" throughout a document, the search and replace function can quickly find all the errors and replace them with the correct spelling.

Serial Interface: The connection between the computer and a peripheral, such as a modem or printer, in which information is transmitted one bit at a time, in series. Alternative to parallel interface.

Software: The programs that make the computer perform. Word-processing software is a type of applications software, where the program is written for a specific, practical application.

Sorting: The ability of a computer, with appropriate software, to arrange records in alphabetical or numerical order.

Spelling Checkers: Programs that automatically search through your file and flag misspellings. The spelling checker contains a dictionary against which words in your file are compared.

Split Screen: A feature of many word-processing programs that allows the operator to divide the screen into two sections and simultaneously work on different documents, or different parts or drafts of the same document, in each section.

Subscript: A character printed one-half vertical space below a line, such as the 2 in H_2O. The ability to print subscripts is a combined function of the software and the printer.

Superscript: A character printed one-half vertical space above a line, such as the 2 in 3^2_seq9. Especially useful in footnoting. The ability to print superscripts is a combined function of the software and the printer.

Synchronous Communications: As opposed to asynchronous communications, the movement of data over transmission lines in blocks defined by a single "start" and "stop" signal.

Terminal: A keyboard and monitor, or a keyboard and printer, that is hooked up to an external computer.

Terminal Emulator: A type of software that enables a word processor or microcomputer to act like a terminal in sending or receiving information over phone or data lines to or from another computer (usually a mainframe which is designed to communicate with external terminals.)

Text Editing: The range of functions in which characters, words, lines, sentences, and paragraphs can be changed, deleted, or moved. Text editing is a major part of word processing, which also includes printing and filing functions.

Typeover: *See Overtyping.*

Underscoring: The ability to underline words. Underscoring is a combined function of the software and printer.

User: The operator of the word-processing system.

Wild Card: A technique that allows you to use a special character, such as the question mark or back slash, to indicate to the computer that it can equal any character. For example, if you were searching through your documents for all occurrences of "counselor," "counselors", and "counseling," you could indicate this by using "counsel?" If the question mark is recognized as a wild card, the computer would find all those words.

Winchester Disk Drive: Another name for the most popular type of hard disk drive.

Windowing: A technique in which the screen is divided into several windows which allow you to simultaneously view different documents or files. For example, windowing may allow you to see an accounting statement in one window, a mailing list in another, and a form letter in a third; information from all of which can be combined in the final document.

Word Processing: The application of computer processing to the inputting, editing, and printing of text documents.

Word Wrap: A feature of many word-processing programs in which the end of one line and the beginning of the next is determined automatically while typing input, and carriage returns are automatically inserted between words.

Index